Outdoor Cookbook

By the Editors of Southern Living

Menus adapted from Southern Living® *Outdoor
Cookbook*, copyright© 1973 Southern Living
Books.

Library of Congress Catalog Number: 86-60696
ISBN: 0-8487-0702-8

Manufactured in the United States of America

First Printing 1986

Cover credit: Photographer, Jim Bathie; Food
Stylist, Sara Jane Ball

Cover: *Shrimp en Brochette, Fruit Salad Delight,
and Grilled Corn with Bacon provide a delicious
alternative to traditional outdoor fare. Seafood
Dream Dinner menu begins on page 90.*

Contents

Introduction

Except for rain, nothing can dampen spirits at an outdoor cookout. The pleasure of cooking outdoors is not limited to a few short months when the weather is agreeably warm. There are times in every month of the year that meals can be cooked outdoors, even though it may be too cold to eat outdoors. In fact, many of the recipes in this book were prepared during February. Hospitality and the perfect recipe can easily be blended for successful outdoor cooking all year long.

In the good old days, most outdoor meals consisted of wieners and marshmallows—appetizing but humdrum after a while. Now, with gas and electric grills, charcoal smokers, and hibachis, you can cook Glazed Pork Loin, Shrimp en Brochette, and Lobster Luau with side dishes like Celery Amandine and Orange Lotus Blossom. . . . And smoke needn't get in your eyes.

Often the backdrop of nature saves you the trouble of decorating. You can enjoy the out-of-doors, while savoring the smell and taste of delicious food. Let nature provide the relaxed atmosphere; you provide the appetite.

Outdoor Menus

Combinations for a barbecue meal are purely a matter of preference, and there are as many possibilities as there are recipes. Preferences may vary within a neighborhood, or even within a family. Some prefer to cook the meat outdoors, prepare the vegetables and salad indoors, and assemble it all together for the "come and get it" signal. Others prefer to cook every single item outdoors, and it *is* possible to cook meat, vegetables, and bread on the grill, quite successfully.

We see no reason why you should use these menus as suggested if there happens to be a particular food your family doesn't like. We've selected foods that "go together," but there's no bound rule and you may well prefer some substitutions. Be daring enough to make changes if you find a vegetable dish with the lamb menu that you would like to use with your beef main course. Use our menus as we have suggested, or make substitutions and combinations for your own special pleasure. Whatever your choice, we hope we will have had a part in making your outdoor meals more creative and more enjoyable.

Rolled Rib Roast on Spit

Dinner for Eight

Rolled Rib Roast on Spit

Grilled Rice with Olives

Okra-Tomato Casserole

Fresh Spinach-Mushroom Salad

Grilled Biscuits

Fresh Peach Ice Cream

Rolled Rib Roast on Spit

1 (3- to 4-pound) boneless rolled
 rib roast
¼ cup port wine
½ teaspoon dry mustard
1 teaspoon brown sugar
¼ teaspoon black pepper
 Dash garlic powder

2 tablespoons salad oil
¼ cup catsup
1 tablespoon
 Worcestershire sauce
1 teaspoon freshly squeezed
 lemon juice
 Dash paprika

Have roast tied tightly at meat counter. Center securely on spit of rotisserie and place over low heat of grill. Cook slowly for 30 minutes. Combine other ingredients in small saucepan; heat just to boiling point. Brush on roast every 15 minutes. Use a meat thermometer to cook meat to desired doneness. It will take about 1 to 1½ hours to reach the rare stage. Yield: 8 servings.

Grilled Rice with Olives

2⅔ cups cooked rice
2⅔ cups water
 4 tablespoons minced onion
 1 teaspoon salt
¼ teaspoon pepper
 2 teaspoons prepared mustard

½ teaspoon hot sauce, or 2
 teaspoons Worcestershire sauce
 4 tablespoons chili sauce
 4 tablespoons butter
 6 tablespoons water
½ cup sliced stuffed olives

Double a large sheet of heavy-duty aluminum foil; fit foil into 2-quart dish to form a pouch. Combine all ingredients in foil except olives. Seal tightly and remove foil from dish. Place on grill over hot coals. Cook for approximately 20 minutes. Open foil and toss rice with fork just before serving. Add olives and stir. Yield: 8 servings.

Okra-Tomato Casserole

2 cups okra, cut into
½-inch pieces
4 to 5 tomatoes, peeled and cut
into small wedges; or 1½ cups
drained canned tomatoes
1 pod green hot pepper,
minced (optional)

½ cup water (omit water if
using canned tomatoes)
Salt and pepper to taste
1 large onion, chopped
1 tablespoon butter
or margarine

Combine all ingredients and cook over medium heat until vegetables are tender. Serve hot. Yield: 8 servings.

Fresh Spinach-Mushroom Salad

1 pound fresh spinach
½ pound fresh mushrooms
Grated rind of 1 lemon

¼ cup salad oil
Juice of 1 large lemon

Tear well-washed spinach into bite-size pieces and put in a large bowl. Wash mushrooms, cut in halves and slice; add to spinach. Combine grated lemon rind, salad oil, and lemon juice. Just before serving, pour over spinach-mushroom mixture and toss gently to coat. Yield: 8 servings.

Grilled Biscuits

(page 33)

Fresh Peach Ice Cream

(page 39)

Your Guest List

When making a guest list, a thoughtful hostess should include persons that have something in common, people she feels will be compatible even though they may not know each other well. If views of a certain person are distasteful to the group as a whole, it would be wise to exclude him from a small gathering. He will probably feel more comfortable invited to a larger party where the guest list would be varied.

Churrasco Dinner

Dinner for Six

Churrasco

Celery Amandine

Summertime Garden Vegetable Casserole

Zesty Salad

Pumpkin Pudding

Churrasco

1¼ cups butter, divided
¼ teaspoon rosemary
1 (3-inch thick) sirloin steak or chuck roast
2 cups finely chopped green onions

1½ teaspoons salt
1 tablespoon freshly ground black pepper
1 cup white wine
½ cup wine vinegar

Combine 3 tablespoons melted butter and rosemary; baste steak once or twice with this mixture while broiling it. (Broil steak to desired degree of doneness.) Melt remaining butter and sauté green onions until just soft. Add rest of ingredients; bring to boil, then lower heat and simmer 5 minutes. Cut steak into diagonal slices and let stand in sauce for a few minutes before serving. Yield: 6 servings.

Celery Amandine

½ cup butter, divided
4 cups celery, diced
Salt and pepper to taste
2 tablespoons finely chopped fresh chives

2 tablespoons grated onion
1 cup blanched, chopped almonds
½ teaspoon finely chopped garlic (optional)
2 tablespoons dry white wine

Melt ¼ cup butter in saucepan; add celery, salt, and pepper and blend well. Cover pan and cook over low heat until celery is tender. Stir frequently while cooking to prevent scorching; add chives and onion. Melt remaining butter in a heavy pan; add blanched almonds and cook over medium heat until brown. Add garlic and wine; cook for 1 minute. Pour over celery and serve immediately. Yield: 6 servings.

Summertime Garden Vegetable Casserole

½ cup butter
1 cup sliced onions
1 clove garlic, minced
2 yellow squash, cut into
½-inch pieces
1 medium eggplant, peeled and
cut into ½-inch pieces

½ cup all-purpose flour
2 green peppers, chopped
2 tomatoes, cut into wedges
1 teaspoon salt
¼ teaspoon oregano
⅛ teaspoon celery salt
⅛ teaspoon pepper

Melt butter in large skillet; sauté onion and garlic until tender. Dredge squash and eggplant in flour to coat lightly. Add squash, eggplant, and green pepper to onions. Cover and simmer for 30 minutes. Add tomatoes, salt, oregano, celery salt, and pepper. Simmer an additional 20 minutes. Yield: 6 to 8 servings.

Zesty Salad

1 onion, thinly sliced and
separated into rings
4 well-ripened tomatoes, sliced
½-inch thick
½ teaspoon salt
¼ teaspoon sugar
Fresh ground black pepper

1 tablespoon chives
1 tablespoon basil
1 tablespoon dill
1 teaspoon celery seed
¼ cup commercial French dressing

Place onion rings and tomato slices on large platter. Sprinkle each slice with salt, sugar, pepper, chives, basil, dill, and celery seed. Top with French dressing. Cover salad with foil and refrigerate about 3 hours to blend flavors. Yield: 6 servings.

Pumpkin Pudding

1½ cups milk
½ cup brown sugar, firmly packed
¼ teaspoon freshly grated
orange peel
¼ teaspoon ground ginger

½ teaspoon ground cinnamon
½ teaspoon salt
3 eggs, slightly beaten
1 cup cooked pureed pumpkin or
canned pumpkin

Combine milk, brown sugar, orange peel, ginger, cinnamon, and salt. Stir thoroughly and add eggs and puréed pumpkin; blend well. Beat vigorously until mixture is smooth. Pour into a greased, shallow 1½-quart baking dish. Place the dish in a large pan in the middle of the oven; pour enough boiling water into the pan to come halfway up the sides of the baking dish. Bake at 350° for about 1¼ hours, or until a knife inserted in the center of the pudding comes out clean. Remove the baking dish from the water; cool the pudding to room temperature before serving or refrigerate at least 3 hours, or until thoroughly chilled. Pudding may be made in six 4-ounce individual glass molds. If cooked in molds, bake at 350° for about 40 minutes, or until firm. Yield: 6 servings.

How To Save Refrigerator Space

Use insulated ice chests to keep bottled drinks and other items cold. This saves refrigerator space. Have plenty of ice on hand!

Pool Party Dinner

Dinner for Eight

Charley-bobs

Oven-Cooked French-Fried Potatoes

Grilled Vegetables

Tossed Salad with French Dressing

Garlic Toast

Chocolate Supreme

Charley-bobs

**4 pounds sirloin steak, 2
inches thick**

**3 pound slice center-cut ham,
2 inches thick**

Cut sirloin steak and ham into 2-inch cubes. Alternate the two meats on metal skewers, and cook on grill over medium heat to desired doneness. Yield: 8 servings.

Oven-Cooked French-Fried Potatoes

**3 pounds frozen French-
fried potatoes**

2 tablespoons salt

Place potatoes in a single layer on a cookie sheet. Bake at 400° for 10 minutes, stir once, then bake 10 minutes longer. Sprinkle with salt and serve at once. Yield: 8 servings.

Grilled Vegetables

**Yellow squash, cut into 2-
inch slices
Small whole onions
Carrots, cut into 1- to
2-inch slices**

**Zucchini squash, cut into
2-inch slices
Green pepper strips (optional)**

Select the vegetables preferred by guests, or have a dish of prepared raw vegetables and let guests make and cook their selection. Put vegetables on skewers and cook over medium heat until vegetables are done.

Meat Temperature

Meat should be at room temperature before it is put on the grill or rotisserie.

Tossed Salad with French Dressing

4 to 6 cups salad greens, torn into
    bite-size pieces
1 cup fresh spinach, torn into
    bite-size pieces
1 cup chopped celery
½ cup diced carrots

½ cup onion rings
½ cup coarsely chopped
    green pepper
1 cup cauliflowerets
    Commercial French dressing

Prepare vegetables and dry well. Cover and chill until just before serving. When ready to serve, add desired amount of French dressing, gently toss and serve at once. Yield: 8 servings.

Garlic Toast

(page 41)

Chocolate Supreme

5 (1¼-ounce) chocolate bars
⅓ cup butter
3 egg yolks, beaten
½ cup powdered sugar
½ cup chopped nuts

3 egg whites, beaten to
    soft peaks
2½ cups crushed vanilla wafers
1 quart vanilla ice
    cream, softened

Melt chocolate bars in top of double boiler; add butter and egg yolks and let mixture come to a boil. Cool. Add powdered sugar, nuts, and beaten egg whites; stir until well-blended. Spread 1½ cups vanilla wafer crumbs in bottom of 9-inch square pan. Cover with softened vanilla ice cream. Pour cooled chocolate mixture over ice cream. Top with remaining cup of vanilla wafer crumbs. Freeze until ready to serve. Yield: 8 to 10 servings.

Watch that Grill!

When you start to barbecue, stay with it. Dripping fat from the meat can start a flame which can cremate a piece of meat very quickly. Get an easy chair, a cold drink, a bottle of water to put out flames of your charcoal fire, and settle down by the grill to keep a watchful eye on the meat as it cooks. If fire is too hot, lower the firebox or raise the grill, if they're adjustable. Move food to edge of grill away from intense heat. If fire is too cool, tap the ash off the briquettes since it acts as an insulator. Lower the grill nearer the heat, if possible.

Sukiyaki Cookout

Dinner for Six to Eight

Sukiyaki

Brown Rice

Mandarin Salad

Frozen Lemon Sherbet Pie

Sukiyaki

2 **pounds sirloin tip, cut into**
  ¼ - x 2-inch diagonal strips
2 **onions, thinly sliced**
½ **cup bean curd (optional)**
6 **green onions including**
  tops, chopped
6 **ribs Chinese celery or cabbage**
2 **cups mushrooms, thinly sliced**

1 **pound spinach, cut into 1-inch strips**
2 **cups bean sprouts**
3 **tablespoons peanut oil**
½ **cup soy sauce**
½ **cup beef broth**
3 **tablespoons brown sugar**
½ **teaspoon monosodium glutamate**
  Chopped green onions

Have all ingredients at room temperature. Cut all vegetables into uniform shape and thickness. Slice green onions and celery diagonally, and cut mushrooms so each slice forms a ''T''. Divide all meat and vegetables into two equal portions (half of recipe fits well in skillet). Combine peanut oil, soy sauce, beef broth, brown sugar, and monosodium glutamate; blend well to make sauce in which to cook meat and vegetables. Pour half of sauce in skillet; add beef slices and cook the meat over medium heat without browning it (about 3

minutes). Push meat aside in skillet; add a vegetable and cook a short time; push this vegetable aside in pan. Continue to add a little sauce when needed in cooking remainder of vegetables. Vegetables should retain their color and crispness. Total cooking time takes about 20 minutes. This one-dish meal can be cooked at the table in an electric skillet or wok, or an iron skillet over a hibachi. Serve over brown rice. Garnish with chopped green onions. Yield: 6 to 8 servings.

Brown Rice

2 **(10½-ounce) cans beef broth**
3 **cups water**
1 **teaspoon salt**

2 **cups brown rice**
  Toasted sesame seeds

Combine beef broth, water, and salt; cook over medium heat until mixture boils. Slowly stir in rice. Cover and cook over low heat for 50 to 60 minutes. Uncover for last 5 minutes

of cooking and sprinkle with sesame seeds. Yield: 6 to 8 servings.

Note: To be authentic, serve a raw egg over each plate of rice and spoon Sukiyaki over egg.

Cutting Sticky Foods

To cut sticky foods, such as marshmallows, use a pair of kitchen shears and dip them in a cup of water frequently while cutting.

Mandarin Salad

3 (11-ounce) cans mandarin
  orange sections, drained
3 bananas, sliced

½ cup grated coconut
  Commercial Italian dressing
  Toasted sesame seeds

Combine mandarin oranges, bananas, and coconut; add a small amount of Italian dressing and toss lightly. Sprinkle with sesame seeds. Yield: 6 to 8 servings.

Frozen Lemon Sherbet Pie

½ cup sugar
3 egg yolks
3 tablespoons freshly squeezed
  lemon juice

  Pinch salt
1 tablespoon grated lemon rind
½ pint whipping cream, whipped
3 egg whites, stiffly beaten
  Commercial crumb crust

Cook sugar, egg yolks, lemon juice, salt, and rind in top of double boiler until thick, stirring constantly. Cool. Fold in whipped cream and stiffly beaten egg whites. Pour mixture into cooled Crumb Crust. Freeze until ready to serve. Yield: 1 (9-inch) pie.

Avoid Collection of Fat on Fire

Make every effort to prevent a burst of flames from touching the meat being cooked on the grill. Before meat is put on the grill, trim off all excess fat. When using charcoal, be sure that all lighter fluid has burned off before putting meat on grill. If you are using a portable grill, tilt slightly to allow some of the fat drippings to run to one side. Keep a squirt bottle of water handy to put out flames when using a charcoal fire.

Barbecued Steak Dinner

Dinner for Eight

Steak à la Henry Bain

Chinese Vegetable Casserole

Mimosa Salad

Sinful Apple Pie

Steak à la Henry Bain

1 (12-ounce) bottle chili sauce
1 (14-ounce) bottle catsup
1 (10-ounce) bottle steak sauce
1 (10-ounce) bottle
   Worcestershire sauce

1 (17-ounce) bottle chutney,
   finely chopped or put
   through blender
   Hot sauce to taste
3 to 4 pounds sirloin steak

Combine first six ingredients and mix well. This makes enough sauce for several "cookings"; it stores well in refrigerator and is better after flavors have had time to blend.

Put steak in hinged basket on grill over low heat; baste with sauce as meat cooks. Yield: 1 quart sauce; steak to serve 8.

Chinese Vegetable Casserole

1 (15-ounce) can
   asparagus, drained
1 (16-ounce) can tiny
   peas, drained
1 (16-ounce) can mixed Chinese
   vegetables, drained
1 (16-ounce) can bean
   sprouts, drained
1 (2-ounce) jar
   pimiento, chopped

1 (3-ounce) can French-
   fried onions
1 cup nuts, chopped
2 hard-cooked eggs, chopped
1 (10¾-ounce) can cream of
   mushroom soup
½ cup margarine, melted
   Salt and pepper to taste
1 cup breadcrumbs
1 cup shredded Cheddar cheese

Combine all vegetables, nuts, eggs, and mushroom soup. Place in casserole dish. Pour margarine over mixture; add salt and pepper. Top with breadcrumbs and cheese. Bake at 350° for 30 minutes. Leftover casserole will keep in refrigerator. Yield: 8 to 10 servings.

Grilling on a Windy Day

When grilling on a windy day, use aluminum foil as a shield for grill. By using long sheets of foil, partially cover the food to speed up the cooking time.

Mimosa Salad

½ cup salad oil
2 tablespoons wine vinegar
½ teaspoon salt
   Dash pepper

⅔ clove garlic, finely minced
2 quarts crisp salad greens
3 hard-cooked eggs,
   finely chopped

Combine oil, vinegar, salt, pepper, and garlic in jar with a tightly fitted lid. Shake and pour over greens in salad bowl. Sprinkle egg on top. Yield: 8 servings.

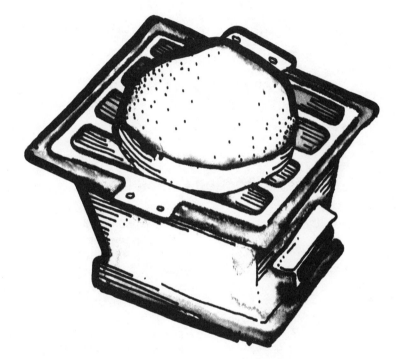

Sinful Apple Pie

¾ cup quick-cooking oats
1 cup all-purpose flour
1 cup brown sugar

½ cup margarine, melted
4 cups apples, pared and sliced

Combine oats, flour, brown sugar, and margarine; mix with apples. Put in 10-inch piepan; bake at 350° for 25 minutes. Yield: 1 (10-inch) pie.

When To Turn Steaks

The correct time to turn steaks is when droplets of red juice appear on the uncooked side. Use tongs or asbestos gloves when turning meat on the grill. Do not pierce meat with a fork, for this allows juice to run out of meat.

Chuck Roast in Deluxe Dinner

Dinner for Six to Eight

Hot Barbecued Chuck Roast

Eggplant Casserole Delight

Fresh Green Beans

Sliced Tomatoes and Green Peppers

Toasted English Muffins

Heavenly Hash Dessert

Hot Barbecued Chuck Roast

2 tablespoons salad oil
½ cup finely chopped onion
¼ cup finely chopped
   green pepper
2 tablespoons brown sugar
1½ cups catsup
   Dash hot sauce

2½ tablespoons cider vinegar
½ teaspoon garlic salt
½ teaspoon salt
1 (3- or 4-pound) chuck roast

Heat salad oil in small skillet; sautè chopped onion and green pepper until limp. Stir in brown sugar, catsup, hot sauce, vinegar, garlic salt, and salt. Bring to a boil, lower heat, and simmer for 10 minutes.

Place roast in hinged basket or place on grill over low heat for 10 minutes; turn and cook 10 minutes on other side. Begin brushing sauce on roast and turn often. Use meat thermometer to cook to desired doneness. Yield: 6 to 8 servings.

Eggplant Casserole Delight

1 (1½-pound) eggplant
3 medium onions, chopped
1 cup water
2 tablespoons butter or
   margarine, melted

2 egg yolks, beaten
1 teaspoon salt
½ cup dry breadcrumbs
½ cup water
½ cup grated Parmesan cheese

Pare eggplant and cut in small pieces. Boil eggplant and onions in 1 cup water until tender, stirring occasionally. Drain and mash; stir in butter, egg yolks, salt, breadcrumbs, and water. Spoon mixture into a greased 1½-quart casserole dish. Bake at 350° for 20 minutes. Sprinkle grated Parmesan cheese on top and bake an additional 10 minutes. Yield: 6 servings.

Fresh Green Beans

**2 pounds fresh green
  beans, cut-up**

**3 cups water
  Fatback or bacon strips**

Place green beans in large saucepan. Add water and fatback or bacon strips for seasoning. Cook, covered, over medium heat until beans are barely tender, about 45 minutes. Drain before serving. Yield: 8 servings.

Toasted English Muffins

(page 70)

Heavenly Hash Dessert

2 apples, diced
**1 (8¼-ounce) can sliced
  pineapple, drained and chopped**
½ cup maraschino cherries
2 bananas, sliced

**2 oranges, peeled, sectioned,
  and cut-up**
½ cup chopped pecans
2 cups miniature marshmallows
1 cup sweetened whipped cream

Mix fruits, pecans, and marshmallows. Stir in whipped cream and chill thoroughly before serving in chilled dessert dishes. Yield: 10 to 12 servings.

Hostess Helper Ideas

If guests want to help you with the meal, give them the tidy jobs, such as setting tables, putting out flower arrangements, or lighting lamps. If you have done all these jobs beforehand, suggest that they just be "company" and talk with other guests or visit with you while you finish up the last-minute chores.

Cook-In, Eat-Out Patio Dinner

Dinner for Six to Eight

Gazpacho

Company Best Meatballs

Rice Casserole

or

Green Bean Casserole

Nine-Day Slaw

Corn Sticks

Pineapple-Cream Cheese Pie

Gazpacho

1 (10½-ounce) can tomato soup
5 cups water
1 cup vegetable juice
¼ cup minced green pepper
¼ cup minced celery
1 tablespoon commercial
   Italian dressing
1 small onion, minced
½ teaspoon salt
⅛ teaspoon black pepper
   Dash garlic salt, hot sauce, and
   Worcestershire sauce
½ medium cucumber, thinly sliced

Put soup in 3-quart saucepan; stir in water, bring to a boil, and simmer for about 5 minutes. Pour into large bowl and allow to chill. Add all other ingredients except sliced cucumber. Put into a jar, seal, and chill thoroughly. When thoroughly chilled, add cucumber slices and serve in chilled glasses or mugs. Yield: 6 to 8 servings.

Company Best Meatballs

1 egg
¾ cup milk
1½ cups breadcrumbs
1½ pounds ground chuck
2 tablespoons Worcestershire sauce
1 teaspoon salt
⅛ teaspoon pepper
⅛ teaspoon red
   pepper (optional)
2 tablespoons shortening
1 (10¾-ounce) can golden
   mushroom soup
⅔ cup water

Combine egg and milk; beat slightly. Add breadcrumbs and stir until moistened. Add meat, Worcestershire sauce, salt, and pepper. Mix well. Shape into small meatballs and brown in shortening. Pour off any accumulated fat. Combine soup and water. (Do not use cream of mushroom soup.) Pour over meatballs. Cover and simmer for 30 minutes. Yield: 24 meatballs.

Rice Casserole

½ cup margarine, melted
1 cup uncooked rice
1 (10½-ounce) can beef consommé
1 (10½-ounce) can onion soup
2 tablespoons Worcestershire sauce
⅛ to ¼ teaspoon red
   pepper (optional)

Combine margarine and rice in skillet; cook over low heat until rice is lightly browned. Pour into 2-quart baking dish. Add remaining ingredients. Stir lightly with a fork. Cover and bake at 350° for 1 hour. (Do not stir while baking.) Yield: 6 to 8 servings.

Green Bean Casserole

1 (10¾-ounce) can cream of
   mushroom soup
   Dash pepper
1 teaspoon soy sauce (optional)
2 (16-ounce) cans green
   beans, drained
2 (3-ounce) cans French-
   fried onions
½ cup shredded Cheddar cheese

Combine soup, pepper, and soy sauce. Place beans in casserole dish in layers with soup mixture and 1 can onions. Cover and bake at 350° for 20 minutes. Sprinkle with remaining onions and cheese. Bake 5 minutes longer. Yield: 6 to 8 servings.

Nine-Day Slaw

1 medium cabbage, shredded
2 stalks celery, diced
2 medium onions, diced
1 green pepper, diced
1 cup sugar
1 cup salad oil
1 cup cider vinegar
1 tablespoon salt
2 tablespoons sugar
   Pimiento (optional)

Combine cabbage, celery, onion, and green pepper; add 1 cup sugar and blend well. Combine remaining ingredients and bring to a boil, stirring constantly. Pour dressing over cabbage mixture immediately and allow to cool. Cover and store in refrigerator. Slaw will be stay fresh and crisp for 9 days. (Chill at least 1 day before serving.) Yield: 6 to 8 servings.

Don't Overcook

When cooking a combination of foods together, as in stews with assorted vegetables or a fish stew with different fish and shellfish, always add those foods that require the longest cooking time first, and add others later.

Corn Sticks

1½ cups milk
2 eggs
4 tablespoons shortening, melted
1½ cups plain cornmeal

½ cup all-purpose flour
2 teaspoons salt
1 tablespoon baking powder
2 tablespoons sugar (optional)

Combine milk and egg; beat slightly. Add shortening. Combine dry ingredients; add to milk mixture. Stir only until moistened. Pour into preheated, greased cornstick pans; bake at 450° about 10 minutes or until golden brown. (Muffin pans or skillet may be used.) Yield: 6 to 8 servings.

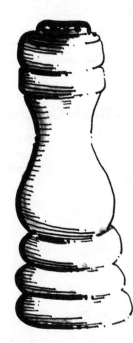

Pineapple-Cream Cheese Pie

1 (14-ounce) can sweetened
    condensed milk
¼ cup freshly squeezed lemon juice
1 (3-ounce) package cream
    cheese, softened

1 (8½-ounce) can crushed
    pineapple, drained
1 (9-inch) graham cracker shell

Combine condensed milk and lemon juice; add cream cheese and beat mixture until smooth. Fold in pineapple. Pour mixture into prepared crumb crust. Chill 4 to 5 hours before serving. Yield: 1 (9-inch) pie.

Organize Your Grocery List

After deciding on the menu for an outdoor party, divide the list into two parts: things to buy early and store, and the perishables that have to be purchased the day of the party.

Hamburger Specials

Dinner for Six

Hamburger Specials
Barbecued Beans
Sour Cream Cole Slaw
Hot Hamburger Buns
Frozen Lemon Sherbet Pie

Hamburger Specials

1½ teaspoons salt
  Dash pepper
2 pounds ground beef

6 onion slices, very thinly sliced
6 bacon slices

Mix seasonings with ground beef. Divide ground beef to make 12 patties. Make two thin patties (about 4½ inches in diameter) for each burger. Place onion slice between two patties.

Seal edges of patties well. Wrap each patty with bacon slice, fastened with toothpick. Grill each side 6 to 7 minutes for rare hamburgers and 9 to 10 minutes for medium. Yield: 6 patties.

Barbecued Beans

½ cup chopped celery
2 (16-ounce) cans pork and beans
2 (4-ounce) cans Vienna
  sausage, drained

1 cup brown sugar
1 large onion

Spread celery in bottom of a 2½-quart casserole dish. Spoon 1 can of pork and beans over celery. Arrange sausage links on top of beans, and cover with the other can of beans.

Sprinkle brown sugar over top and press onion into center of dish. Bake at 300° about 1 to 1½ hours, or cover and cook on grill for 1 hour. Yield: 6 to 8 servings.

Sour Cream Cole Slaw

1 teaspoon salt
⅛ teaspoon pepper
¼ teaspoon dry mustard
1 tablespoon sugar

2 tablespoons freshly squeezed
  lemon juice
½ cup commercial sour cream
3 cups finely shredded cabbage

Combine seasonings, sugar, and lemon juice with sour cream; blend well. Add to cabbage; toss lightly. Chill. Yield: 6 servings.

Frozen Lemon Sherbet Pie

(page 13)

Best Brisket Barbecue

Dinner for Four to Six

Barbecued Brisket

Stuffed Tomato Salad

Potato Casserole in Foil

Brandy Ice

Barbecued Brisket

1 (4- to 5-pound) boneless
  beef brisket
½ cup grated onion
½ cup vinegar
½ cup catsup
1 cup water
1 tablespoon prepared mustard

1 tablespoon sugar
1½ tablespoons
  Worcestershire sauce
½ teaspoon black pepper
½ teaspoon paprika
1 clove garlic, crushed

Put beef brisket in large glass or enameled dish. Combine other ingredients for marinade and pour over brisket. Refrigerate overnight. The next day, remove brisket from marinade; place on double thickness of heavy-duty aluminum foil. Pour marinade over brisket. Partially close top and place on grill over very low heat. Cook until desired doneness. Yield: 4 to 6 servings.

Alternate method: Brisket may be spread with salt, pepper, and liquid smoke and cooked directly on grill. When meat is done, slice and place in hot sauce mixture.

Stuffed Tomato Salad

1 (10-ounce) package frozen
  English peas
6 medium tomatoes
  Lettuce leaves

Creamy commercial salad dressing

Cook peas according to package directions. Scoop out centers from tomatoes, leaving only the shell. Stuff tomatoes with peas and chill until serving time. Serve on lettuce leaves and top with your favorite dressing (onion, Green Goddess, or blue cheese). Yield: 6 servings.

Storing Charcoal

Store briquettes or charcoal in a dry place because they absorb moisture and cause the fire to kindle slowly.

Potato Casserole in Foil

**6 medium potatoes, peeled and
   cut into ⅜-inch slices
4 medium onions, peeled
   and sliced
   Salt and pepper to taste**

**8 ounces Cheddar cheese, cut
   into cubes
6 bacon strips, fried crisp
   and crumbled**

Place potato and onion slices on heavy-duty aluminum foil. Season with salt and pepper. Sprinkle with cheese cubes and crumbled bacon. Wrap foil tightly. Cook about 1 hour on grill or in covered casserole dish at 375° for 1 hour. Yield: 4 to 6 servings.

Brandy Ice

**1 quart vanilla ice cream,
   slightly thawed
3 ounces brandy**

1¼ ounces crème de cacao

Combine all ingredients in blender and blend until smooth. Serve as a milk shake. Yield: 4 to 6 servings.

Locating a Portable Grill

The grill can be adapted to any location, depending on the crowd and recreational plans. The pit should be placed parallel with the wind as nearly as possible. This will give a good drawing effect, and the smoke will travel away from the cooks who are tending the meat on the grill. Avoid using a grill in an enclosed area. Fires produce carbon monoxide which can be extremely hazardous if it accumulates in closed porches or garages. Keep party decorations away from the grill.

Flank Steak Special

Dinner for Six

Barbecued Flank or Skirt Steak

Special Hot Potato Salad

Assorted Relishes

Celery Bread

Fresh Fruit

Quick Brownies

Barbecued Flank or Skirt Steak

1 (2- to 3-pound) flank or
skirt steak
Salt and pepper to season
1 to 2 cloves garlic, crushed

1½ teaspoons oregano, crushed
2 tablespoons vinegar
4 tablespoons salad oil

Put steak in a flat glass baking dish. Combine salt, pepper, garlic, oregano, vinegar, and salad oil. Pour mixture over steak and let it marinate in this mixture for 1 hour. Remove from marinade and broil over high heat for 3 or 4 minutes; turn and cook on other side for 3 or 4 minutes. Carve into thin diagonal slices. Yield: 6 servings.

Special Hot Potato Salad

10 to 12 small new potatoes
6 strips bacon
1 medium onion, chopped fine
¼ cup vinegar

6 scallions or 2 green peppers,
finely chopped
Salt and pepper to taste
3 hard-cooked eggs, cut
into quarters

Cook potatoes in boiling salted water until just tender. Plunge into cold water, peel, and thinly slice. While potatoes are cooking, fry bacon until crisp. Remove bacon, crumble it, and set aside. Add chopped onion to bacon drippings and cook until tender. Add vinegar, scallions, salt and pepper, and blend. Pour this sauce over potatoes and mix lightly. Garnish with hard-cooked eggs. Yield: 6 servings.

Serve All Guests at One Time

To be sure all guests are served at the same time, it's better to cut a very large steak into eight pieces than to cook only four steaks at a time on the grill.

Celery Bread

⅓ to ½ cup butter or
   margarine, softened
½ to 1 teaspoon celery seed

⅛ teaspoon salt
1 (1-pound) loaf unsliced bread

Combine softened butter or margarine, celery seed, and salt; mix well and set aside. Remove crusts from three sides and both ends of an unsliced loaf of bread. Slice lengthwise and crosswise into 2-inch squares, not cutting through to bottom crust. Spread butter between squares and over top and side of bread. Bake at 300° for 20 to 25 minutes. Remove from oven, wrap in heavy-duty aluminum foil, and keep warm on grill. Yield: 6 to 8 servings.

Quick Brownies

(page 86)

Cooking Steaks

Turn steaks only once, always using tongs. A fork will pierce the meat and let juice escape. To prevent steak from curling, score or slit the fat on edge at about 1½-inch intervals before placing it on the grill. Be careful not to cut into the meat, or you will lose precious juice. It is not necessary to score steaks that are thicker than 1½ inches.

Meal from the Coals

Dinner for Six to Eight

Chuck Roast on Coals

Summer Squash and Corn

Spiced Peach Salad

Garlic Bread

Vanilla Ice Cream

Chuck Roast on Coals

**1 (3- or 4-pound) chuck roast,
   3 inches thick**
2 large cloves garlic, crushed

½ cup salad oil
¼ cup Dijon mustard
1 cup ice cream salt

Spread roast with crushed garlic. Combine salad oil and mustard, and brush this mixture on roast to completely cover it. Put ice cream salt over oil-mustard mixture and press into meat to coat it. Let stand awhile, then repeat applications of oil-mustard and salt. Let roast sit for 2 hours, adding as much salt as roast will take to form a crust.

Brush gray ash from a flat bed of charcoal briquettes, and lay roast directly on coals. A piece of aluminum foil may be placed on top of roast. Cook about 20 minutes, then move to another bed of coals from which ash has been brushed. Cook 20 minutes. Check for desired doneness, and cook longer if necessary. To serve, cut in strips across the grain. Yield: 6 to 8 servings.

Summer Squash and Corn

¼ cup chopped onion
**2 tablespoons butter or
   margarine, melted**
   Corn cut from 4 medium ears, or
   1 (10-ounce) package frozen corn
3 medium tomatoes, diced

**4 medium zucchini squash,
   thinly sliced**
½ teaspoon sugar
1 teaspoon salt
¼ teaspoon ground black pepper
¾ teaspoon ground oregano

Sauté onion in melted butter or margarine. Add other ingredients, stir until mixture comes to a boil; cover saucepan and cook over low heat for 20 minutes. Adjust seasonings and serve hot. Mixture will be thick. Yield: 8 servings.

Spiced Peach Salad

1 (29-ounce) can peach halves,
  undrained
1 teaspoon ground cinnamon
½ teaspoon ground cloves
1 teaspoon ground allspice

¾ cup brown sugar
½ cup cider vinegar
1 (3-ounce) package cream cheese,
  softened
  Half-and-half

Drain peaches, reserving juice. Mix spices, brown sugar, and vinegar with ¾ cup reserved juice. Bring to a boil, reduce heat and simmer for 5 minutes. Pour mixture over peach halves while hot. Let sit for several hours or overnight. Before serving, combine cream cheese and enough half-and-half to make a smooth mixture. Place a teaspoon of this mixture in center of each peach half. Yield: 7 to 8 servings.

Garlic Bread

(page 82)

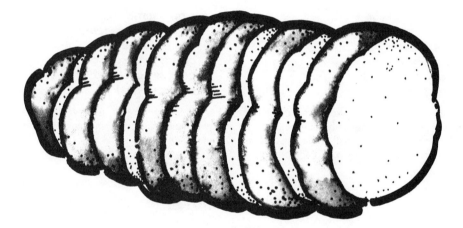

Vanilla Ice Cream

1½ cups milk
¾ cup sugar
⅛ teaspoon salt

2 or 3 egg yolks
1 tablespoon vanilla extract
1 pint whipping cream, whipped

Scald milk over low heat. Add sugar and salt; stir until dissolved. Beat egg yolks and add hot milk mixture slowly. Beat until well-blended. Cook in top of double boiler until thick and smooth. Chill and add vanilla extract. Whip cream and fold into custard mixture. Freeze in electric or hand-turned freezer. Yield: 1½ quarts.

Quick Barbecue

For a quick barbecue dinner, slice leftover cold roast beef or pork, mix your favorite barbecue sauce, and cook on the grill, basting generously with the sauce as meat cooks.

Teriyaki Beef Special

Dinner for Eight

Teriyaki Beef Sticks
Marinated Vegetable Platter
Spinach Madeleine
Garlic Toast
Peach Meringue
Marlene's Punch

Teriyaki Beef Sticks

1½ cups soy sauce
½ cup salad oil
1 cup vinegar
1 cup water
1 cup brown sugar
1 teaspoon salt

5 cloves garlic, minced
1 large onion, chopped
⅓ cup chopped fresh gingerroot,
  or 5 tablespoons ground ginger
3 pounds boneless beef roast
  or round steak

Combine all ingredients except meat to make marinade. Slice meat into 1-inch strips that are ⅛ inch thick. Skewer meat strips accordion-style on bamboo sticks, using 4 inches of meat per stick. Marinate in sauce 4 hours or overnight. Grill about 15 minutes, turning often. Yield: 8 servings.

Marinated Vegetable Platter

(page 33)

Spinach Madeleine

2 (10-ounce) packages frozen
  chopped spinach
2 tablespoons chopped onion
4 tablespoons butter, melted
2 tablespoons all-purpose flour
½ cup vegetable liquor
½ cup evaporated milk

½ teaspoon pepper
¾ teaspoon garlic salt
¼ teaspoon salt
1 teaspoon Worcestershire sauce
1 (6-ounce) roll of Jalapeño
  cheese, cut into small pieces
  Buttered breadcrumbs (optional)

Cooling a Charcoal Fire

Small amounts of crushed ice will cool a charcoal fire quickly.

Cook spinach according to package directions; drain and reserve liquor. Sauté onion in butter until tender. Add flour, stirring until blended and smooth. Slowly add liquor and milk, stirring constantly; cook until smooth and thick. Add pepper, garlic salt, salt, Worcestershire sauce, and cheese; stir until cheese is melted. Combine with spinach. Put into a 2-quart casserole dish; top with breadcrumbs. Bake at 350° for about 30 minutes or until bubbly. Yield: 8 servings.

Garlic Toast

(page 41)

Peach Meringue

2 cups canned peaches, drained
1 tablespoon freshly squeezed
   lemon juice
1 envelope unflavored gelatin
½ cup cold water
2 egg whites
1 (4½-ounce) container frozen
   whipped topping, thawed

Cut peaches into pieces and put into blender. Add lemon juice and blend 4 seconds. Soften gelatin in cold water and heat until dissolved. Add to fruit and blend 2 seconds. Let stand 5 minutes. Add 1 unbeaten egg white; blend 10 seconds. Add second egg white; blend 3 seconds. Put 2 tablespoons whipped topping into eight sherbet glasses; pour peach mixture on top. Top with another spoonful of whipped topping. Chill overnight. Yield: 8 servings.

Marlene's Punch

1 quart orange sherbet
1 (46-ounce) can
   pineapple juice
Gin to taste

Soften sherbet with pineapple juice, mixing slowly with a big spoon or whip. Add gin and mix slowly. Serve in chilled glasses. Yield: 8 servings.

When Stocking the Bar

For a small gathering (20 or so) ask your co-host or a friend to tend the bar for the first hour, after which time he may leave his post to join other guests, leaving bottles, ice, and mixers out so guests may help themselves to refills.

When buying liquor remember that there are seventeen 1½-ounce drinks in a fifth of liquor; roughly 200 drinks to a case (12 bottles to a case). To be on the safe side, allow three drinks per guest. Although some guests will have only one drink, it's better to have too much than not enough.

If your party is a sizeable one, you'll undoubtedly have some non-drinkers. For them, it's thoughtful to provide a large pitcher of chilled fruit juice and an assortment of carbonated drinks.

Make ice a week before the party and store the cubes in plastic bags in the freezer. If you don't have a freezer, buy the ice the afternoon before the party and keep it in a tub out of sight.

Provide plenty of napkins, olives, cherries, lemon and orange wedges, and also a tray or table for used glasses.

Lamb-on-the-Spit

Dinner for Eight

Kraut Barbecued Lamb

Fresh Tomato Salad

Corn-Stuffed Peppers

Grilled Biscuits

Fresh Summer Fruit

Picnic Lemonade

Kraut Barbecued Lamb

1 cup kraut juice
1 medium onion, sliced
2 cloves garlic, cut in halves
¼ teaspoon celery seed
¼ teaspoon ground black pepper
1 (5- to 6-pound) leg of lamb
⅓ cup honey
1 teaspoon freshly squeezed lemon juice

Combine kraut juice, onion, garlic, celery seed, and pepper. Put lamb in shallow glass dish and pour marinade over meat; cover dish and chill for 1 day, turning occasionally. Skewer lamb on rotisserie spit. Place spit about 8 inches above heat, and cook for 30 minutes per pound for medium doneness. Blend honey and lemon juice, heat and brush on lamb during the last 30 minutes of cooking time. Yield: 8 servings.

Fresh Tomato Salad

12 ripe tomatoes, chopped
4 fresh green onions, chopped
1 large green pepper, chopped
¼ cup vinegar
¼ teaspoon salt
2 teaspoons sugar
½ teaspoon basil

Combine tomatoes, onions, and pepper. Mix vinegar, salt, sugar, and basil, and stir into vegetable mixture. Cover dish and refrigerate until ready to serve. Yield: 8 to 10 servings.

Corn-Stuffed Peppers

8 medium green peppers
1 teaspoon salt
4 cups corn, cut from cob; or
   frozen corn, thawed
1⅓ cups diced fresh tomatoes
1½ teaspoons instant minced onion

¼ teaspoon ground black pepper
¼ teaspoon garlic powder
1 teaspoon chili powder
4 tablespoons all-purpose flour
2 tablespoons butter or
   margarine, melted

Slice tops from green peppers; carefully remove seeds and membranes. Put in a saucepan with salted water; cover and boil for 5 minutes. Carefully remove from water with a slotted spoon.

Combine other ingredients, and spoon into peppers. Place filled peppers in a shallow baking dish, and bake at 375° for about 25 to 35 minutes, or until done. Yield: 8 servings.

Grilled Biscuits

(page 33)

Picnic Lemonade

½ cup light corn syrup
½ cup sugar
⅔ cup water
2 tablespoons grated lemon rind

1¼ cups freshly squeezed
   lemon juice
7 cups water
Cherries and lemon slices

Combine corn syrup, sugar, water, and lemon rind. Bring mixture to a boil, and allow to boil for 5 minutes. Strain and cool. Place ice cubes in large pitcher; add cooled mixture, lemon juice, and water. Garnish with cherries and lemon slices. Yield: 10 servings.

No-Fuss Vegetable Tip

Frozen vegetables are delicious cooked on the grill. Remove from package, dot with butter, season, and wrap securely (while still frozen) in heavy-duty aluminum foil. Turn package once during cooking process, which takes about 30 to 35 minutes.

Lamb Kabob Dinner

Dinner for Six to Eight

Cold Avocado Soup

Lamb Kabobs

Polynesian Sweets

Marinated Vegetable Platter

Grilled Biscuits

Ice Cold Watermelon Wedges

Cold Avocado Soup

1 **large avocado**
1 **(10½-ounce) can consommé**
   Several dashes hot sauce
3 **tablespoons freshly squeezed**
   lemon juice

1 **pint commercial sour cream**
   Chopped parsley or chives

Peel and pit avocado; cut into small pieces and put into blender with consommé, hot sauce, and lemon juice. Blend well. Add sour cream and blend just to mix well. Chill in refrigerator for several hours and serve cold. Garnish with chopped parsley or chives. Yield: 8 (6-ounce) servings.

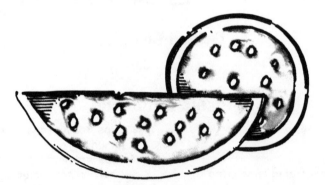

Lamb Kabobs

1 **(3- to 4-pound) loin of lamb**
1 **cup red wine**
¼ **cup olive oil**

3 **cloves garlic, crushed**
   Salt and pepper to taste
   Dash oregano

Cut lamb into 2-inch squares. Combine wine, olive oil, garlic, salt, pepper, and oregano for marinade and put in glass or enameled dish. Place lamb in marinade, cover, and refrigerate 2 or 3 days. Remove from marinade, place on desired number of skewers, and cook over low heat about 15 to 20 minutes, turning frequently. Brush kabobs often with marinade as meat is cooking. Yield: 6 to 8 servings.

Polynesian Sweets

2 **sweet potatoes, peeled and cut**
into ½-inch slices
2 **bananas, cut into**
½-inch slices
1 **cup pineapple tidbits, drained**

1 **cup miniature marshmallows**
Margarine
Brown sugar
Almonds, diced

Place sweet potato slices on large piece of aluminum foil. Top with banana slices, pineapple, and marshmallows. Dot with margarine; sprinkle with brown sugar and diced almonds. Wrap tightly in foil. Grill 10 to 15 minutes. Yield: about 6 to 8 servings.

Marinated Vegetable Platter

6 **medium carrots**
1 **small head cauliflower**
½ **cup wine vinegar**
¾ **cup salad oil**
½ **teaspoon garlic powder**
½ **teaspoon prepared mustard**

¼ **teaspoon salt**
½ **teaspoon basil leaves, crushed**
1 **tablespoon minced onion**
Salad greens
Cherry tomatoes

Peel carrots and cut into halves; boil in lightly salted water until just tender. Cook cauliflower in boiling water until just tender. Remove both pans from heat, drain and chill thoroughly. Combine vinegar, salad oil, garlic powder, mustard, salt, basil leaves, and minced onion. Stir or shake to blend well. Divide dressing and pour half over the drained carrots and half over the drained cauliflower. Seal containers and let sit in refrigerator overnight.

To serve, put salad greens on outer layer of platter, layer carrot strips and cherry tomatoes inside salad greens, and put cauliflower in center of platter. Serve with remaining marinade. Yield: 6 to 8 servings.

Grilled Biscuits

2 **cups all-purpose flour**
3 **teaspoons baking powder**
1 **teaspoon salt**

⅓ **cup shortening**
About ⅔ cup milk
4 **tablespoons margarine, melted**

Combine flour, baking powder, and salt in large bowl. Cut in shortening with two knives or a pastry blender until mixture resembles coarse cornmeal. Add milk and mix lightly. Turn out onto lightly floured board or pastry cloth, and roll to ½-inch thickness. Cut with a 2-inch biscuit cutter. Brush tops with melted margarine, and place biscuits directly on grill over low heat. Cover with a sheet of aluminum foil. Bake about 10 minutes, or until biscuits are browned. If you prefer the tops browned, turn biscuits once. Yield: 16 (2-inch) biscuits.

Using Skewers

Select long, sturdy skewers that reach completely across the grill. Place foods on skewers with some space between them to allow for heat penetration and thorough basting. Unless some vegetables are parboiled, they may require a longer cooking time than meat cubes; therefore you may want to put them on separate skewers. When using bacon strips, string in and out, along chunks of food on skewer. Unpainted wire coat hangers or small green sticks make handy skewers.

Lamplighter Luau

Dinner for Eight

Rumaki

Roast Leg of Lamb

Buttermilk Rice

Easy Cole Slaw

Carrot Sticks

Celery Bread

Watermelon

Tropical Treat Cubes

Rumaki

10 **canned water chestnuts, halved**
5 **chicken livers, cut**
   into quarters

10 **slices bacon, halved**
¼ **cup soy sauce**
2 **tablespoons brown sugar**

Wrap a piece of water chestnut and chicken liver in a half slice of bacon; fasten with a toothpick. Combine soy sauce and brown sugar; chill appetizers in this mixture for ½ hour. Spoon marinade over appetizers occasionally; drain. Broil 3 inches from heat until bacon is crisp, turning once. Yield: 20 appetizers.

Roast Leg of Lamb

1 **(4- to 5-pound) boned leg**
  of lamb
1 **(10-ounce) package frozen**
  asparagus, thawed
½ **cup chopped parsley**
½ **cup finely chopped celery**
½ **cup lime juice, divided**
1 **tablespoon dry white wine**

½ **teaspoon salt**
⅛ **teaspoon pepper**
¼ **teaspoon garlic powder**
18 **fresh mint leaves, chopped**
  Salt
3 **tablespoons créme de**
  menthe liqueur
½ **cup salad oil**

Remove all fell (tissue-like covering) from lamb. Thaw asparagus and combine it with parsley, celery, 1 tablespoon lime juice, wine, salt, pepper, garlic powder, and 9 chopped mint leaves. Spread stuffing mixture on lamb and roll up, tying every 2 inches with strong string. With a sharp knife, make incisions in lamb and insert remainder of mint leaves. Rub some salt on surface. Place lamb securely on rotisserie; cook over medium heat 2 hours for well-done lamb. During last 15 minutes of cooking, baste meat with mixture of remaining lime juice, créme de menthe, and salad oil. Remove to hot platter and let set 10 minutes before carving. Drizzle some of basting sauce on slices after carving. Yield: 8 to 10 servings.

Buttermilk Rice

1½ cups cooked rice
½ cup cornmeal
3 cups buttermilk
¾ teaspoon soda

1 teaspoon salt
3 eggs, slightly beaten
3 tablespoons margarine, melted
¼ to ½ cup sugar (optional)

Combine all ingredients in large bowl in order given. Pour into greased, shallow 2-quart casserole dish and bake at 350° for 30 minutes, or cook in foil. Cut eight pieces of heavy-duty aluminum foil into 12-inch squares. Place a square of foil in small bowl, patting it into shape of bowl. Place a serving of rice mixture in each foil packet and seal tightly. Place foil packets on low-heat part of grill. Cook until slightly firm, about 30 minutes, moving packets about occasionally. Fold back foil and use as individual serving dishes. Yield: 8 servings.

Easy Cole Slaw

3 cups finely shredded cabbage
¼ cup chopped green pepper

Slaw Dressing

Toss shredded cabbage with ice cubes; refrigerate until ready to serve. Remove ice and drain. Add green pepper. Toss with Slaw Dressing. Yield: 8 servings.

Slaw Dressing

⅓ cup salad dressing
1 tablespoon wine vinegar
2 tablespoons peanut oil

1 teaspoon salt
½ teaspoon celery seed

Combine salad dressing, vinegar, peanut oil, salt, and celery seed. Mix well and pour over Cole Slaw. Yield: ½ cup.

Celery Bread

(page 25)

Tropical Treat Cubes

2 bananas, mashed
1 (6-ounce) can orange juice
1 (6-ounce) can pineapple juice
   Juice of 1 lime

Juice of 1 lemon
⅔ cup sugar
   Mint leaves

Combine mashed bananas, orange, pineapple, lime, and lemon juices with sugar. Mixture can be well-blended in blender. Pour mixture into refrigerator tray and freeze into cubes. Serve in sherbet glasses and garnish with mint leaves, or serve on tray, piercing each cube with a toothpick. Yield: 8 servings.

Deluxe Lamb Steak Dinner

Dinner for Four

Pepper Lamb Steaks

Herbed Vegetable Kabobs

Curried Fruit

Garlic-Dill French Bread

Pineapple Sherbet

Mint Punch

Pepper Lamb Steaks

4 lamb steaks, cut ½-inch thick
Unseasoned meat tenderizer

Seasoned salt
1 tablespoon peppercorns

Moisten lamb and sprinkle with meat tenderizer, following label directions. Sprinkle lightly with seasoned salt. Place peppercorns in a plastic bag and crush with a rolling pin. Press onto each side of steaks. Place steaks on grill about 6 inches above hot coals. Grill, turning once; cook 12 minutes for medium doneness or cook until meat reaches desired degree of doneness. Yield: 4 servings.

Herbed Vegetable Kabobs

8 small new potatoes
2 medium zucchini squash
2 medium yellow squash
8 large fresh mushrooms

2 large tomatoes
1 large green pepper
¼ cup butter, melted
2 teaspoons herb seasoning

Scrub potatoes and cut off a band of skin around the middle of each. Trim zucchini and yellow squash but do not pare; cut each into 1-inch thick slices. Parboil potatoes in boiling salted water for 15 minutes; drain. Combine zucchini and yellow squash and parboil in boiling salted water for 5 minutes; drain. Wash mushrooms and cut into halves lengthwise. Cut each tomato into 8 wedges. Cut pepper into ¼-inch thick slices. Thread potatoes and squash alternately onto four long skewers; thread mushrooms, tomato wedges, and green pepper strips, alternately, onto four more long skewers. Combine butter and seasoning; brush part of mixture over vegetables. Place potato-squash skewers on grill about 6 inches above heat. Grill, turning and brushing several times with butter mixture, for 10 minutes. Place mushroom-tomato skewers on grill. Continue grilling for 10 minutes or until potatoes and squash are tender and mushrooms and tomatoes are heated through. Yield: 4 servings.

Curried Fruit

1 (17-ounce) can mixed
   fruit, drained
1 (8½-ounce) can pineapple
   tidbits, drained
1 (8¾-ounce) can apricot
   halves, drained

¼ cup margarine, melted
¾ cup brown sugar
1½ teaspoons curry powder

Place drained fruit in shallow casserole dish. Combine margarine, brown sugar, and curry powder; pour over fruit. Bake at 300° for 30 minutes. Serve hot. Yield: 4 to 6 servings.

Garlic-Dill French Bread

(page 101)

Pineapple Sherbet

1 quart milk
1½ cups sugar
½ cup freshly squeezed
   lemon juice

1 cup drained crushed pineapple

Scald milk. Cool. Add sugar, lemon juice, and pineapple. Freeze in freezer section of refrigerator or in electric or hand-turned freezer. Yield: 2 quarts.

Mint Punch

18 to 20 sprigs fresh mint
1 cup sugar
1 quart boiling water
1 cup plus 2 tablespoons frozen
   lemonade concentrate
1 quart orange juice

1⅓ cups pineapple juice
2 cups club soda
2 cups ginger ale
12 sprigs mint
½ cup thin lemon slices

Wash 18 to 20 sprigs mint; put into large saucepan with 1 cup sugar and 1 quart boiling water. Simmer, uncovered, for 10 minutes. Chill. When ready to serve, strain mint syrup and add chilled lemonade, orange juice, pineapple juice, club soda, and ginger ale. Serve with mint sprigs and lemon slices. Yield: 4 to 6 servings.

When Using Mushrooms

If your grocer does not stock fresh mushrooms, here's a guide for substituting canned ones:
   1 (6- or 8-ounce) can is the equivalent of 1 pound fresh.
   1 (3- or 4-ounce) can is the equivalent of ½ pound fresh.

Should a recipe call for fresh mushrooms by measure instead of by weight, here's your guide:
   For 1 quart (or 20 to 24 medium mushroom caps), substitute 1 (6- to 8-ounce) can.
   For 1 pint (or 10 to 12 medium mushroom caps), substitute 1 (3- to 4-ounce) can.

Chicken Surprise Dinner

Dinner for Eight to Ten

Chicken Surprise
Shirley's Potato Salad
Asparagus Deluxe
Fresh Peach Ice Cream

Chicken Surprise

4 **chickens, cut into halves**
½ **cup olive oil**
   Salt and pepper to taste
   Paprika
   Juice of 8 large lemons
1¾ **cups wine vinegar**

4 **teaspoons light brown sugar**
2 **large pieces candied
   ginger, minced**
3 **tablespoons candied orange
   peel, minced**
4 **teaspoons rosemary**

Rub chicken with olive oil; sprinkle with salt, pepper, and paprika. Combine remaining ingredients and mix well; use sauce to baste chicken frequently while cooking over medium heat. Turn chicken and continue to baste often. Yield: 8 to 10 servings.

Shirley's Potato Salad

8 **medium potatoes**
2 **tablespoons wine vinegar**
4 **tablespoons olive oil**
2 **teaspoons salt (or to taste)**
2 **teaspoons white pepper
   (or to taste)**

1 **cup chopped celery**
1 **small purple onion, chopped**
4 **hard-cooked eggs**
10 **small Spanish olives, sliced**
8 **dark olives, sliced**
¾ **cup mayonnaise**

Cook potatoes until tender. While still hot, dice and coat potatoes with the vinegar and olive oil. Add salt and pepper. Allow to cool. Stir in the celery, onion, eggs, and olives. Add mayonnaise. Cover and allow flavors to blend. Yield: 8 to 10 servings.

Asparagus Deluxe

6 tablespoons butter, melted
6 tablespoons cornstarch
2 (10½-ounce) cans
  asparagus spears

Milk
4 hard-cooked eggs, thinly sliced
2 cups shredded Cheddar cheese
Buttered breadcrumbs

Combine butter and cornstarch; stir over medium heat until mixture is smooth and bubbly. Drain asparagus and reserve juice; add enough milk to reserved juice to make 3 cups. Add milk mixture to sauce; cook, stirring constantly, until mixture begins to thicken. Layer asparagus, eggs, cheese, and sauce in a greased 1½-quart casserole dish. Repeat layers. Top with buttered breadcrumbs. Bake at 325° for 30 minutes. Yield: 8 to 10 servings.

Fresh Peach Ice Cream

1½ cups sugar
2 tablespoons all-purpose flour
½ teaspoon salt
3 eggs, beaten
1 quart whole milk, divided

½ pint whipping cream
1 tablespoon vanilla extract
6 cups mashed fresh peaches
1 cup sugar

Combine 1½ cups sugar, flour, and salt; add eggs and blend well. Add 1 pint milk and cook slowly over low heat until slightly thickened. Cool. Add whipping cream, remainder of milk, vanilla, and peaches which have been sweetened with 1 cup sugar. Pour into electric or hand-turned freezer and freeze until firm, using 8 parts crushed ice to 1 part ice cream salt. Yield: 1 gallon.

For a Successful Chicken Barbecue

1. Organize a time schedule and follow it through for a perfect family or community chicken barbecue.

2. Allow time for all off-odors to leave the source of heat before starting to cook.

3. Remember advance insect control is a must for everyone's comfort and good sanitary practices.

4. In case of rain, have a small tarpaulin and four posts available for an emergency tent over the grill.

5. If fire becomes too hot, turn chickens more often and mop with sauce.

6. Place all chickens with skin-side up to begin cooking. Unless a hinged basket is used, be very careful to check that all chickens are turned at one time.

7. Be liberal with barbecue sauce. Be sure to have enough to serve as a side dish with the cooked chicken.

8. Barbecued chicken, packed tightly in boxes lined with heavy-duty aluminum foil will keep hot for an hour or longer.

9. Consider the serving and keep all food in a sanitary condition.

10. Careful cleaning of the grounds is a must after any serving of foods. Be sure that all fires are extinguished before leaving.

Barbecued Chicken Deluxe

Dinner for Eight

Barbecued Chicken Deluxe

Candied Sweet Potatoes

Cabbage Casserole

Garlic Toast

Rich Peach Ice Cream

Barbecued Chicken Deluxe

½ cup dry white wine
½ cup salad oil
1 teaspoon chopped chives

2 tablespoons chopped parsley
3 (2-pound) chickens, cut-up
   Tomato Wine Sauce

Combine wine, salad oil, chives, and parsley; marinate chicken at room temperature for 1 hour in this mixture. Turn chicken in the marinade several times. Broil or grill for 30 minutes or until done, turning frequently and basting with Tomato Wine Sauce. Yield: 8 servings.

Tomato Wine Sauce

1 cup canned tomatoes
1 cup dry white wine
1 cup thinly sliced okra
1½ cups beef bouillon
½ cup finely chopped celery
1 tablespoon freshly squeezed
   lemon juice
¼ teaspoon hot sauce
2 cloves garlic, minced
1 teaspoon salt

1 teaspoon chili powder
¼ cup Worcestershire sauce
½ cup salad oil
1 tablespoon sugar
1 bay leaf, crumbled
½ teaspoon oregano
½ teaspoon basil
½ cup finely chopped onion
   Freshly ground black pepper

Combine all ingredients and bring to a boil. Reduce heat and simmer for 45 minutes. Strain or put through blender. Serve with barbecued chicken. This sauce is also excellent with ham, pork, or lamb. Yield: about 6 cups.

Candied Sweet Potatoes

4 **medium sweet potatoes, unpeeled**
⅓ **cup sugar**
⅓ **cup brown sugar, firmly packed**

¾ **cup orange juice**
1 **tablespoon cornstarch**
¼ **cup butter or margarine**

Cook potatoes in boiling salted water until almost tender. Remove from water and cool. Remove skin and cut potatoes in quarters; place in a flat 1½-quart baking dish. Combine other ingredients in a saucepan and bring to a boil. Pour over potatoes, cover and bake at 375° for 15 minutes. Remove cover and cook an additional 10 minutes. Yield: 8 servings.

Cabbage Casserole

1 **medium cabbage**
4 **tablespoons butter, melted**
4 **tablespoons all-purpose flour**
½ **teaspoon salt**
¼ **teaspoon pepper**
2 **cups milk**

½ **green pepper, chopped**
½ **medium onion, chopped**
⅔ **cup shredded Cheddar cheese**
½ **cup mayonnaise**
3 **tablespoons chili sauce**

Cut cabbage in wedges; boil in salted water until tender, about 15 minutes. Drain cabbage and place in 13- x 9- x 2-inch casserole dish. Combine butter and flour in saucepan over low heat; stir until smooth and bubbly. Add salt, pepper, and milk. Stir constantly over medium heat until sauce is smooth and thick. Pour sauce over cabbage in casserole dish and bake at 375° for 20 minutes. Combine green pepper, onion, cheese, mayonnaise, and chili sauce; mix well and spread over cabbage. Bake at 400° for 20 minutes. Yield: 8 to 10 servings.

Garlic Toast

½ **cup margarine**
1 **tablespoon grated Parmesan cheese**
1 **teaspoon garlic powder**

2 **tablespoons processed sharp cheese**
1 **(1-pound) loaf French-style bread**

Combine margarine, Parmesan, garlic powder, and sharp cheese; whip until light and fluffy. Cut bread into 4-inch slices, then split slices. Toast outer crust, then spread cut-side with cheese mixture. Return to oven and toast until mixture is bubbly and edges are golden brown. Yield: 6 to 8 servings.

Rich Peach Ice Cream

1 **quart whipping cream**
2½ **cups sugar, divided**

Pinch salt
3 **cups crushed ripe peaches**

Scald cream and half of sugar in top of double boiler. Stir well to dissolve sugar. Add salt. Mash peaches to a purée or blend well in blender. Add remaining sugar to peaches, stirring well to dissolve sugar. Place cream in electric or hand-turned freezer and freeze to a thick mush. Stir in peaches and complete freezing. Remove dasher and pack with more ice and salt. Allow ice cream to stand an hour or two before serving. Yield: 2 quarts.

Cook-Your-Dinner-at-Night

Dinner for Eight to Ten

Smoked Turkey
Orange Candied Sweet Potatoes
Tomato Sauce Piquante
Tossed Spinach-Orange Salad
Butterscotch Crunch Squares

Smoked Turkey

1 (12- to 16-pound) turkey   **Seasoned salt**

Rub turkey with seasoned salt. Put 10 pounds of charcoal briquettes in charcoal pan of smoker; light fire. Let fire burn 10 to 15 minutes and add 6 to 8 blocks of hickory to fire. Place water pan in smoker and fill with water. Place grill in smoker, put turkey on and cover with top. It will take 10 to 12 hours to cook. Do not peek at meat, but allow it to cook slowly to perfection without being disturbed. You may wish to put the turkey in the smoker at night before you go to bed, and it will be juicy and tender the next morning. Yield: 8 to 10 servings.

Orange Candied Sweet Potatoes

4 medium sweet
  potatoes, unpeeled
⅓ cup brown sugar,
  firmly packed

⅓ cup sugar
¾ cup orange juice
Dash salt
¼ cup butter or margarine

Cook potatoes in boiling salted water until barely soft. Remove from water and cool. Remove skin and cut into quarters or ¾-inch slices. Place in a flat 1½-quart baking dish. Combine other ingredients in small saucepan and bring to a boil; pour over potatoes in baking dish. Cover dish and bake at 375° for 25 minutes; uncover dish and bake an additional 15 to 20 minutes, or until syrup has cooked down and potatoes are glazed. Yield: 8 servings.

Tomato Sauce Piquante

8 ripe tomatoes
1 cup salad oil
4 tablespoons tarragon vinegar
4 tablespoons chopped parsley
¼ cup sliced green onions

2 teaspoons chopped fresh thyme,
  or ½ teaspoon dry thyme
1 teaspoon salt
¼ teaspoon pepper
1 clove garlic, minced

Peel and quarter tomatoes; put into a deep bowl. Combine other ingredients in a jar and mix well. Pour over tomatoes, cover bowl, and chill several hours or overnight. When ready to serve, drain and serve tomatoes. Dressing may be stored and used again. Yield: 8 servings.

Tossed Spinach-Orange Salad

3 cups fresh spinach, torn
   into small pieces
3 medium oranges, sectioned

1 tablespoon sugar
   Salt to taste
¼ cup French Dressing

Combine spinach, orange sections, sugar, and salt in a large bowl. Add ¼ cup (or more, if desired) French Dressing and toss. Yield: 6 to 8 servings.

French Dressing

1 teaspoon salt
¼ teaspoon sugar
3 tablespoons freshly squeezed
   lemon juice

¼ cup catsup
½ cup salad oil
1 (3-ounce) package cream
   cheese, softened (optional)

Combine the first five ingredients in a pint jar; shake well and let sit several hours before using. The softened cream cheese may be added to dressing just before serving. Yield: 1 cup.

Butterscotch Crunch Squares

1 cup all-purpose flour
¼ cup quick-cooking oats
¼ cup brown sugar, firmly packed
½ cup butter or margarine
½ cup chopped nuts

1 (12-ounce) jar butterscotch
   ice cream topping
1 quart vanilla ice
   cream, softened

Combine flour, oats, and brown sugar; cut in butter until mixture resembles coarse crumbs. Stir in nuts. Pat mixture into a 13- x 9- x 2-inch baking pan. Bake at 400° for 15 minutes. Stir mixture while still warm to crumble; cool, Pat three-fourths of crumb mixture in bottom of 9-inch square pan; drizzle half of ice cream topping over crumbs in pan. Stir ice cream to soften; spoon carefully over topping mixture. Drizzle with remaining topping; sprinkle with remaining crumb mixture. Freeze. Yield: 8 to 10 servings.

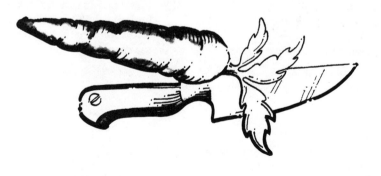

Basting Tip

Food may be basted during the entire cooking time or during the last half hour, depending on the ingredients in the sauce. A small paintbrush or long handled cotton dishmop works well for basting and brushing on sauce. Sauces containing sugar (or ingredients that burn readily) should be applied during the last 15 to 30 minutes of cooking time.

Tailgate Picnic

Picnic for Twelve

Gingered Chicken

Tangy Baked Beans

Tarragon-Tuna Eggs

Crisp Relish

Prune Cake

Spiced Coffee or Lemon-Orange Drink

Gingered Chicken

1½ cups all-purpose flour
1½ tablespoons ground ginger
2 teaspoons salt

3 teaspoons pepper
2 (2½-pound) chickens, cut-up
Shortening for frying

Combine flour, ginger, salt, and pepper in paper bag. Place chicken pieces in bag; shake until chicken is coated with flour. Remove chicken pieces to dry; replace in flour and shake again. Heat shortening in iron skillet and fry chicken until brown on both sides. Yield: 12 servings.

Tangy Baked Beans

1 (1-pound 15-ounce) can pork
and beans, drained
1 (16-ounce) can pork and
beans, drained
½ cup brown sugar, firmly packed

3 tablespoons sherry
1½ tablespoons orange-flavored
instant breakfast drink
1½ teaspoons instant coffee
½ teaspoon salt

Drain beans. Add rest of ingredients and mix well. Spoon into 2-quart casserole dish. Bake at 350° for about 45 minutes. Yield: 12 servings.

Tarragon-Tuna Eggs

12 hard-cooked eggs
1 (7-ounce) can tuna
½ cup mayonnaise
1 teaspoon vinegar

½ teaspoon crushed
tarragon leaves
½ teaspoon salt

Cut eggs in halves lengthwise. Remove yolks to small bowl and mash well. Drain and flake tuna; mix with egg yolks. Add other ingredients and mix well. Stuff tuna mixture into whites. Refrigerate until time to serve. Yield: 12 servings.

Crisp Relish

4 cups chopped cabbage
1 small onion, chopped
1 medium green pepper, chopped
1 teaspoon turmeric

1 cup vinegar
1 teaspoon salt
1 teaspoon celery seed
1 cup sugar

Combine cabbage, onion, green pepper, and turmeric; mix well. Mix vinegar, salt, celery seed, and sugar; boil for 5 minutes. Pour over the vegetables and mix well. Cool and refrigerate. Yield: 12 servings.

Prune Cake

1 (16-ounce) package dried prunes
1 (18½-ounce) package spiced cake mix

½ cup chopped walnuts
Orange Icing

Cook prunes as directed on package (omit any sugar). Drain and reserve liquid. Chop prunes finely. Make cake as directed, using prune juice in place of water. Fold in 1 cup prunes and walnuts with cake batter. Pour into greased 13- x 9- x 2-inch pan. Bake at 350° for 30 to 40 minutes or until cake tests done. Cool completely. Frost with Orange Icing. Yield: 12 to 15 servings.

Orange Icing

1 (8-ounce) package cream cheese, softened
1½ tablespoons orange-flavored instant breakfast drink

½ cup powdered sugar
1 tablespoon water
Cooked prunes

Combine all ingredients except prunes and mix well. Fold in remainder of cooked prunes. Mix well. Yield: enough icing to cover a 13- x 9- x 2-inch cake.

Spiced Coffee

Hot strong coffee
Grated sweet chocolate

Sweetened whipped cream
Cinnamon stick

Brew coffee to double strength and have other ingredients in small bowls. For each cup, use: 1 soup spoon chocolate and 1 heaping spoon whipped cream. Stir with cinnamon stick and serve in mugs.

Lemon-Orange Drink

3 (6-ounce) cans frozen orange juice concentrate
Cold water
1½ cups fresh or bottled lemon juice

Cracked ice
Lemon slices
Maraschino cherries

Combine concentrate with ½ can less water than called for in directions on can. Add ½ cup lemon juice, mixing well. Pour into glasses filled with cracked ice. Garnish each glass with a lemon slice and a maraschino cherry. Yield: 12 servings.

Easy Barbecued Chicken Dinner

Dinner for Eight

Easy Barbecued Chicken
Onion-Bean Bake
Zucchini and Corn Casserole
Garlic Toast
Five-Cup Salad

Easy Barbecued Chicken

**4 (2- to 2½-pound) fryers,
cut into halves**

**2 to 3 cups commercial
barbecue sauce**

Wash chicken halves and drain well. Place on barbecue grill over low heat with meat-side down; turn after 10 minutes and begin brushing with barbecue sauce. Keep a close watch on chicken so that it does not burn. Baste often and turn often. It will take about 30 to 45 minutes to cook chicken. Yield: 8 servings.

Onion-Bean Bake

**4 wieners, sliced
2 (1-pound) cans pork and beans
1 cup shredded Cheddar cheese
2 tablespoons brown sugar**

**2 teaspoons parsley flakes
½ teaspoon seasoned salt
1 (3-ounce) can French-fried
onion rings**

Combine wieners, beans, cheese, brown sugar, parsley flakes, and seasoned salt. Stir in ½ can of onion rings. Spoon mixture into a greased 1½-quart casserole dish. Bake at 350° for 25 minutes. Sprinkle top with remaining onion rings, and bake 5 minutes longer.

Using the Meat Thermometer

A meat thermometer inserted so that the bulb doesn't touch bone or fat is the most accurate way to test doneness of meat. For a roast, insert thermometer in the center. Beef will be rare when the internal temperature is 140°, medium at 160°, and well-done at 170° For poultry, the thermometer should be inserted in the thickest part of the thigh, close to the body. For ham, place thermometer in the middle of the thickest part of meat. Fresh pork should always be cooked to an internal temperature of 170°.

Zucchini and Corn Casserole

6 medium zucchini squash, sliced
½ cup diced onion
2 tablespoons butter or
   margarine, melted
1 cup cooked cream-style corn
   Dash ground cumin

Dash garlic salt
¼ teaspoon black pepper
½ teaspoon salt
   Dash paprika
¼ cup seasoned croutons
½ cup shredded Cheddar cheese

Sauté squash and onion in melted butter or margarine until tender, stirring constantly. Stir in corn, cumin, garlic salt, pepper, salt, and paprika. Mix well and spoon mixture into a 1½-quart casserole dish. Sprinkle top with seasoned croutons and sprinkle shredded cheese on top. Bake at 300° for 30 minutes. Yield: 6 to 8 servings.

Garlic Toast

(page 41)

Five-Cup Salad

1 cup drained mandarin oranges
1 cup drained pineapple chunks
1 cup miniature marshmallows

1 cup flaked coconut
1 cup commercial sour cream

Combine all ingredients in a large bowl, and stir gently to blend. Cover and place in refrigerator for 3 hours before serving. Yield: 8 servings.

When Is the Chicken Done?

It's easy to tell if chicken is done by twisting the drumstick. If the joint twists out of the socket easily, the meat is done. Be sure to serve the chicken while it is hot, and try to have extra sauce to serve alongside the barbecued chicken.

A Picnic Packed for Two

Crudités

Chicken Liver Pâté

French Bread

Roasted Rock Cornish Hens

Ham and Tomato Open-Faced Sandwiches

Fresh Fruit and Assorted Cheese

Smaland Twists and Chocolate Diagonals

Rhine Wine and Bordeaux Blanc

Crudités

1 carrot
1 stalk celery

Cauliflower
Green pepper

Clean and peel the carrot. Slice into sticks. Clean and slice celery into sticks. Break several cauliflower buds from the head. Clean the interior of a green pepper, then slice in rounds. Crisp the raw vegetables in cold water in the refrigerator overnight or several hours before packing for the picnic. Pack in a plastic container or plastic bag for carrying. Yield: 2 servings.

Chicken Liver Pâté

1 pound fresh chicken livers
½ cup sherry wine
½ cup butter

Salt, pepper, rosemary, and
thyme to taste

Put the fresh chicken livers in a saucepan and add sherry to just cover the livers. Simmer over low heat until done, but not tough. Put in the blender, add butter and seasonings. Blend and pour into ramekins for serving. Yield: about 3 cups.

Roasted Rock Cornish Hens

2 Cornish hens
Rock salt

Brown paper
Salad oil

Clean the hens. Fill the bottom of an earthenware Dutch oven with the rock salt. Place the hens in the Dutch oven and cover with the brown paper which has been greased with the salad oil. Bake at 300° about 1 hour, or until done. Yield: 2 to 4 servings.

Ham and Tomato Open-Faced Sandwiches

1 (½-pound) small loaf brown-
   and-serve bread
½ cup butter or
   margarine, softened
   About 32 cherry tomatoes

1 (14½-ounce) can
   asparagus spears
¼ cup mayonnaise
6 slices baked ham,
   thinly sliced

Bake bread according to package directions. When cool, slice as thin as possible and spread with softened butter. Refrigerate. The hardened butter keeps a moist sandwich topping from making the bread soggy. When the butter has hardened remove from the refrigerator and proceed with the sandwiches.

Using half the loaf of buttered bread, cover each slice with a layer of sliced cherry tomatoes. Lay a spear or two of asparagus across each sandwich. Put the mayonnaise in a plastic container and carry on the picnic. Just before serving, drop a teaspoon on each sandwich. Yield: about 6 to 8 small sandwiches.

Smaland Twists

1 cup butter, softened
½ cup sugar
1 cup commercial sour cream

1 teaspoon soda
3 cups all-purpose flour
   Sugar

Cream butter and ½ cup butter until smooth. Gradually add sour cream. Add soda mixed with small amount of flour. Gradually work in remaining flour. Turn dough onto floured board and work until smooth. Divide dough into 40 equal parts

and roll each piece into a string. Shape into twists. Dip in sugar and bake on greased baking sheets at 475° for about 10 minutes or until light golden. Serve soft; or dry twists at 250°. Yield: 40 twists.

Chocolate Diagonals

1 cup butter or margarine, softened
1 cup sugar
1 egg
⅓ cup cocoa
½ teaspoon vanilla extract

¼ teaspoon soda
2 cups all-purpose flour
½ egg, slightly beaten
¼ cup slivered almonds

Cream butter and sugar; add egg, cocoa, and vanilla extract. Sift soda and flour together and gradually add to butter mixture. Work dough until smooth. Divide dough into three parts. Roll out each part into ½-inch thick

strand. Place on buttered cookie sheet. Brush strands with egg and sprinkle with almonds. Bake at 350° about 10 minutes. Cut strands into ¾-inch diagonals while still hot. Yield: 35 to 40 cookies.

How Many Ice Cubes?

To eliminate the bothersome task of filling and refilling ice trays, make your ice cubes ahead of time and store them in a plastic bag in the freezer. Count on 350 cubes for 50 people, or 7 cubes per person.

Teriyaki Meal From the Grill

Dinner for Four

Chicken Teriyaki

Corn-Okra Special

Island Fruit Salad

Skewered Bread Chunks

Lemon Sherbet

Chicken Teriyaki

⅔ cup soy sauce
¼ cup white wine
2 tablespoons sugar
1 clove garlic, minced

1 tablespoon salad oil
½ teaspoon ground ginger
1 medium-size fryer, cut-up

Combine soy sauce, wine, sugar, garlic, salad oil, and ginger. Marinate chicken in this mixture at least 1 hour or overnight in refrigerator. Chicken may be baked at 325° or on outdoor grill. Baste each piece two or three times while cooking. Yield: 4 servings.

Corn-Okra Special

1 small onion, cut in strips
1 medium green pepper, diced
3 large ears of corn
1 cup fresh okra
1 beef bouillon cube
½ cup boiling water

2 tablespoons butter
  or margarine
  Dash garlic salt
½ teaspoon salt
  Dash white pepper

Prepare onion and green pepper. Remove husks and silks from corn. Cut off kernels with a sharp knife; scrape down with back of knife to remove pulp. There should be about 1½ cups.

Slice okra into ½-inch rounds. Dissolve bouillon cube in hot water and set aside.

Melt butter or margarine in 10-inch skillet. Add onion and green pepper; cook gently, stirring often, until partly tender. Add corn, okra, bouillon, garlic salt, salt, and pepper. Cover tightly and simmer, stirring several times, until corn and okra are tender, about 5 to 10 minutes. Yield: 4 servings.

Tenderizing Meat

Tenderize meat and chicken by rubbing inside and out with lemon juice.

Island Fruit Salad

1 small fresh pineapple
1 small cantaloupe
1 fresh pear
2 bananas
1 cup strawberries

2 oranges
1 cup seedless grapes
Lemon juice
Fruit Dressing

Cut pineapple into chunks, cut cantaloupe into balls, and slice pear, bananas, and strawberries. Section oranges and cut into bite-size pieces; leave grapes whole. Dip all fruits in lemon juice, combine fruits and chill in covered container. Pour dressing over fruit, blend well and serve cold. Yield: 4 generous servings.

Fruit Dressing

½ to ¾ cup orange juice
¼ cup salad oil
1 tablespoon sugar
½ teaspoon salt

½ teaspoon paprika
¼ teaspoon celery seed
½ clove garlic, crushed

Combine all ingredients in jar; shake gently to blend, cover and allow to sit several hours in refrigerator before serving on fruit salad. Yield: 1¼ cups.

Skewered Bread Chunks

1 or 2 cloves garlic, crushed
½ cup butter or
    margarine, melted
2 tablespoons minced
    fresh parsley

1 (1-pound) loaf French bread
3 to 6 tablespoons grated
    Parmesan cheese

Combine garlic, butter, and parsley. Cut French bread in half lengthwise, then crosswise in 2-inch slices. Spread butter on bread and sprinkle with Parmesan cheese. Spear bread on skewers and grill about 5 inches above heated grill for about 5 minutes, or until lightly toasted. Yield: 4 to 6 servings.

Lemon Sherbet

2 (6-ounce) cans frozen
    lemonade concentrate
1¾ cups sugar

¼ teaspoon salt
2 tablespoons grated lemon rind
6 cups evaporated milk

Put lemonade concentrate, sugar, salt, and lemon rind in a large bowl. Beat together until well-blended. Slowly stir in evaporated milk and mix well. Pour mixture into 1-gallon freezer can. Freeze in electric or hand-turned freezer, using a mixture of 8 parts crushed ice to 1 part ice cream salt. When ice cream is frozen, tip freezer to drain off water.

Before opening can, wipe lid carefully. Scrape ice cream off dasher and pack firmly in can. Cover with double thickness of waxed paper and replace lid (fitted with cork or paper plug). Repack with a mixture of 4 parts crushed ice to 1 part ice cream salt. Cover with paper or heavy cloth. Let stand 1½ to 2 hours to ripen. Yield: 1 gallon.

Deluxe Cornish Hen Dinner

Dinner for Six

Stuffed Cornish Hens

Mushroom Potatoes

Pickled Eggs

Wilted Endive Salad

Cheesecake

Stuffed Cornish Hens

6 Cornish hens
½ lemon
2 teaspoons salt
2 teaspoons pepper
12 chicken livers
3 tablespoons butter, melted
6 medium mushrooms, sliced

2 tablespoons butter, melted
½ cup chopped ham
¼ cup chopped toasted almonds
¼ cup butter, melted
¼ cup dry white wine
2 tablespoons red currant jelly

Wash hens; rub cavities with lemon, salt, and pepper. Sauté chicken livers in 3 tablespoons butter; remove from heat and chop very fine. Sauté mushrooms in 2 tablespoons butter; combine livers, mushrooms, ham, and almonds to make dressing. Stuff hens lightly with dressing; skewer the openings and tie legs together. Combine ¼ cup melted butter, wine, and jelly; baste hens with this mixture. Place hens in shallow pan and put in smoker or bake in oven at 350°. Cook until fork-tender, about 45 minutes to an hour, basting frequently. Yield: 6 servings.

Mushroom Potatoes

3 to 4 potatoes, peeled and thinly sliced
1 (10¾-ounce) can cream of mushroom soup

Salt and pepper to taste
Butter
Grated Parmesan cheese

Boil sliced potatoes until about half done. Layer in shallow, buttered casserole dish with mushroom soup; sprinkle lightly with salt and pepper and dot with butter. Top with Parmesan cheese. Bake at 350° for about 30 minutes, or until potatoes are done and soup is bubbly. Yield: 6 servings.

Pickled Eggs

1 (16-ounce) jar pickled beets

6 hard-cooked eggs, peeled

Drain beets and reserve juice. Place beets and eggs in clean glass jar. Heat beet juice and pour over beets and eggs. Cover and let sit overnight. Yield: 6 servings.

Wilted Endive Salad

1 large head endive
5 slices bacon, fried crisp
  and crumbled
1 onion, thinly sliced
¼ cup bacon drippings

½ cup sugar (less if desired)
¾ teaspoon salt
¼ cup vinegar
  Water (optional)

Separate endive and wash thoroughly. Toss with bacon bits and onion slices. Combine bacon drippings, sugar, salt, vinegar, and water; heat until it bubbles and sugar is dissolved. Pour hot dressing over salad greens. Toss thoroughly so greens are wilted. Serve immediately. Yield: 6 servings.

Cheesecake

1 (8-ounce) carton ricotta or
  cottage cheese, drained
½ (8-ounce) package cream
  cheese, softened
1 tablespoon commercial sour cream
2 tablespoons all-purpose flour
¼ teaspoon salt
½ teaspoon vanilla extract

  Rind of ½ lemon, grated
2 egg yolks
2 egg whites
½ cup sugar
1 (8½-ounce) can crushed
  pineapple, drained
  Pastry

Put drained ricotta in blender and blend until smooth. Add cream cheese, sour cream, flour, salt, vanilla extract, lemon rind, and egg yolks to ricotta in blender. Blend until smooth. Beat egg whites with sugar until soft peaks form; fold into cheese mixture. Put crushed pineapple in bottom of baked pastry shell; fill shell with cheese mixture. Bake at 300° for 30 to 45 minutes until cheese sets. Chill before serving. Yield: 6 servings.

Pastry

½ cup plus 2 tablespoons
  all-purpose flour
3 tablespoons sugar

6 tablespoons butter
1 egg, slightly beaten

Combine flour and sugar. Cut in butter with pastry blender until mixture resembles coarse meal. Gradually add egg to dry mixture. Dough will be quite soft. Line bottom and sides of greased 9-inch piepan with pastry. Bake at 300° for 15 minutes. Cool before filling shell. Yield: 1 (9-inch) pie.

Tip for Serving French Bread

Here is a tip for the hostess who has watched guests tugging at French bread trying to break slices away from the bottom, uncut crust.

After preparing the loaf in the usual manner, butter between slices and complete the slicing all the way through the bottom crust. Hold the loaf into shape with your hands. Taking a long skewer, stick it through the loaf, lengthwise, thus holding the loaf firmly in place. Keep the skewer in the loaf throughout the heating process, and just before serving time, slide the slices off the skewer into a basket or onto a platter.

North of the Border Meal

Dinner for Four

Chili con Queso with Corn Chips

Tequila and Tonic

Pollos Rollenos

(Chicken Rolls)

Patatas Mantequilla

(Potatoes in Butter)

Ensalada Mexicana

(Mexican Salad)

Dulce Paraíso

(Paradise Dessert)

Chili con Queso with Corn Chips

3 tablespoons butter
3 tablespoons all-purpose flour
1½ cups milk
1½ cups shredded Cheddar cheese
**1 to 2 (4-ounce) cans green
    chiles, finely chopped***

Dash black pepper
½ teaspoon salt
Dash paprika
¼ teaspoon hot sauce (optional)
Corn chips

Melt butter in 1-quart saucepan over low heat. Add flour and stir until smooth. Cook a few minutes; add milk slowly, stirring to keep mixture free from lumps. Cook and stir until mixture thickens.

Add cheese and chopped chiles (add 1 can and taste before adding second can). Mix well. Remove from heat as soon as cheese melts. Add pepper, salt, paprika, and hot sauce. Serve hot with corn chips. Yield: 2½ cups.

*This sauce is fairly hot with 2 cans of chiles. For those guests too far north of the border, reduce the fire by adding ½ teaspoon sugar.

Note: If by chance there is any left over, this makes a delicious topping over baked potatoes, vegetables, or as a sandwich spread.

Tequila and Tonic

1 jigger tequila
2 ice cubes

Tonic water
Lemon slices (optional)

Put tequila and ice cubes in a 6- or 8-ounce glass. Fill glass with tonic water and serve with a slice of lemon if desired. Yield: 1 serving.

Pollos Rollenos

(Chicken Rolls)

4 whole chicken breasts
2 tablespoons shortening
1 small onion, chopped
2 cloves garlic, minced
3 fresh tomatoes, chopped
3 eggs, beaten

1 cup toasted almonds
1 teaspoon chopped parsley
  Salt to taste
½ cup salad oil
  Juice of 1 lemon
¼ cup water

Remove bones from chicken breasts, leaving each breast in one piece. Set aside. Melt shortening in skillet; sauté onion and garlic until lightly browned. Add chopped tomatoes; stir in eggs and cook until eggs coagulate. Add almonds, parsley, and salt. Remove from heat and cool slightly. Stuff chicken breasts with this mixture; fasten with skewers. Broil over hot coals for 30 minutes, or until chicken is tender, turning frequently. During the last 15 minutes of cooking time, brush chicken with basting sauce made by combining salad oil, lemon juice, and water. Yield: 4 servings.

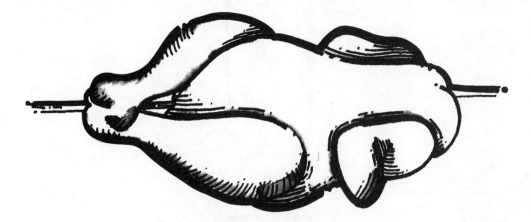

Patatas Mantequilla

(Potatoes in Butter)

4 medium potatoes
4 tablespoons butter or margarine

Salt and pepper

Pare and slice each potato onto a double 12-inch square of heavy-duty aluminum foil. Add 1 tablespoon butter to each packet; sprinkle with salt and pepper. Wrap securely. Cook over hot coals about 1 hour, turning packets frequently. Yield: 4 servings.

Plan Meal Around Meat

Plan your menus to include three or four simple dishes, and think of the entire meal rather than just the meat. Serve vegetables and salads that are compatible with the meat. Desserts may be served, but make them simple.

Since most barbecue meals are rather heavy, many guests do not want dessert; make it a "take your choice" or "take it or not" type dessert.

Ensalada Mexicana

(Mexican Salad)

3 **large green peppers**
1 **medium onion**
4 **medium, ripe tomatoes**
4 **slices bacon**

1 **teaspoon chili powder**
½ **cup vinegar**
   Lettuce leaves

Thinly slice peppers, onion, and tomatoes in a large bowl; mix gently. Cut bacon into 1-inch pieces; cook until crisp in a hot skillet.

Stir in chili powder and vinegar. Bring quickly to a boil and pour over vegetables. Toss gently and serve on lettuce leaves. Yield: 4 servings.

Dulce Paraíso

(Paradise Dessert)

½ **cup sugar**
½ **cup water**
1 **ounce liqueur (any flavor)**
12 **ladyfingers**
2 **cups milk, divided**

2 **tablespoons cornstarch**
3 **eggs, beaten**
¾ **cup sugar**
¼ **pound blanched almonds, ground**
   Ground cinnamon

Boil ½ cup sugar and ½ cup water for 10 minutes. Remove from heat and add liqueur. Place ladyfingers in a 1½-quart glass platter and cover with syrup.

Combine ⅓ cup milk with cornstarch; stir in beaten eggs, mix well and set aside. Heat ¾ cup sugar and remainder of milk; stir in the egg-cornstarch mixture and mix well. Cook slowly, stirring constantly, until mixture thickens. Add ground almonds, remove from heat, cool slightly, then pour over ladyfingers. Sprinkle with ground cinnamon and chill. Yield: 4 to 6 servings.

Disposable Pans

Make disposable pans from heavy-duty aluminum foil for heating vegetables, buns, and other foods on top of grill. Turn up edges for 1½- to 2-inch sides; pinch corners so "pan" won't leak.

Barbecued Chicken Special

Dinner for Six to Eight

Peppered Barbecue Chicken

Cheesy Zucchini Casserole

Rice Salad

Hot Curried Fruit in Foil

Raspberry Delight

Peppered Barbecue Chicken

1 cup salad oil
**2 cups freshly squeezed lemon
  juice or vinegar**

1 cup water
4 tablespoons white pepper
2 to 3 (2½-pound) fryers, cut-up

Combine salad oil, lemon juice, water, and pepper in a large flat dish. Lay chicken pieces in marinade and let sit for at least 2 hours. Remove chicken from marinade and drain carefully. Place in hinged basket on grill over low heat; cook until meat is done, brushing often with marinade, and turning basket often to keep chicken from burning. Chicken should cook about 25 minutes. Yield: 6 to 8 servings.

Cheesy Zucchini Casserole

4 to 6 tender zucchini squash
2 hard-cooked eggs, sliced
2 tablespoons butter or margarine
2 tablespoons all-purpose flour
¼ teaspoon salt
1 cup milk

**½ cup shredded Cheddar cheese
  Red pepper to taste**
**4 to 6 tablespoons
  buttered breadcrumbs**
**¼ cup grated Parmesan or
  Romano cheese**

Wash squash well; split each lengthwise into three pieces; boil in salted water for 5 minutes. Drain well and place in a shallow baking dish; place sliced eggs over squash. Melt butter over low heat; stir in flour and salt until well-blended. Add milk and cook, stirring constantly, until mixture thickens. Add shredded Cheddar cheese and stir until cheese is melted. Pour over squash and eggs. Taste and adjust salt; add red pepper. Top with a mixture of buttered breadcrumbs and sprinkle grated cheese over top. Bake at 375° for 25 to 30 minutes, or until mixture is bubbly and brown. Yield: 6 to 8 servings.

Rice Salad

3 cups cooked rice
6 hard-cooked eggs, chopped
½ cup chopped green pepper
1 bunch green onions, chopped
1 (2-ounce) jar
   pimientos, chopped

1 stalk celery, finely chopped
1 tablespoon freshly squeezed
   lemon juice
   Salad dressing or mayonnaise
   Salt and pepper to taste

Combine rice, eggs, green pepper, onions, pimientos, and celery in a large bowl. Combine lemon juice with just enough salad dressing or mayonnaise to moisten and hold salad together. Add salt and pepper to taste. Yield: 6 to 8 servings.

Hot Curried Fruit in Foil

6 slices canned
   pineapple, drained
1 cup sliced strawberries or
   drained canned whole blueberries

3 tablespoons butter or
   margarine, melted
1½ teaspoons curry powder

Cut 12 (8-inch) squares of heavy-duty aluminum foil. Make a double thickness. Put a slice of pineapple on each of the six packets. Put strawberries or blueberries on top of pineapple slices. Combine melted butter and curry powder and spoon over berries. Wrap packets securely, and place on coolest part of the grill to cook for about 15 minutes, turning packets several times. Yield: 6 servings.

Raspberry Delight

1 (6-ounce) can frozen pink
   lemonade concentrate
   Cold water

1 pint raspberry sherbet
   Whipped topping
   Cherries

Mix lemonade with cold water as directed on can and chill until very cold. Spoon one or two scoops raspberry sherbet in tall glasses and pour lemonade over. Just before serving, add whipped topping, and top with a cherry. (Serve with a straw and a parfait spoon.) Yield: 4 servings; double the recipe to serve 8.

Onion Juice in a Hurry

When you need just a few drops of onion juice for flavor, sprinkle a little salt on a slice of onion and scrape the salted surface with a knife or spoon to obtain the juice.

Oriental Chicken Dinner

Dinner for Eight

Chicken Oriental

Grilled Rice with Olives

Mixed Vegetable Casserole

Sliced Tomatoes

Twenty-Four Hour Salad or Dessert

Chicken Oriental

8 chicken breast halves
½ cup soy sauce
½ cup dry white wine
Juice of 2 limes or 1 lemon

1 clove garlic, crushed
2 teaspoons curry powder
1 teaspoon ground ginger
1 teaspoon minced onion

Wash chicken and dry with paper towels. Combine all other ingredients for marinade. Put chicken in large, flat, glass or enamel dish; cover with marinade and refrigerate overnight, turning chicken several times. Drain and cook on grill about 15 minutes; turn and cook an additional 15 minutes, or until chicken is done, basting often with sauce. Yield: 8 servings.

Grilled Rice with Olives

(page 6)

Using Rack or Grill

Do not put rack or grill over heat until ready to start cooking.

Mixed Vegetable Casserole

2 (10-ounce) packages frozen
  mixed vegetables
1 (10½-ounce) can
  asparagus spears
4 hard-cooked eggs

1 cup mayonnaise
1 small onion, chopped
1 teaspoon dry mustard
1 teaspoon Worcestershire sauce
½ to 1 teaspoon hot sauce

Cook frozen mixed vegetables according to package directions. Cut asparagus spears into small pieces; cook over medium heat until thoroughly heated. Separate cooked egg whites and yolks. Chop cooked egg whites and combine with mayonnaise, onion, mustard, Worcestershire sauce, and hot sauce; blend sauce well and combine with drained cooked vegetables. Put mixture into a greased, flat 2-quart casserole dish and heat to 350° just until mixture begins to bubble. Garnish wtih crumbled egg yolks and serve hot. Yield: 8 servings.

Twenty-Four Hour Salad or Dessert

1 (20-ounce) can pineapple tidbits
1 (1-pound) can pitted
  white cherries
3 egg yolks
2 tablespoons vinegar
2 tablespoons sugar
  Dash salt

1 tablespoon butter or margarine
2 medium oranges, peeled
  and diced
2 cups miniature marshmallows
¼ cup maraschino
  cherries, halved
1 cup whipping cream, whipped

Drain pineapple, reserving 2 tablespoons juice. Drain white cherries and set aside. Beat egg yolks slightly in top of double boiler; add reserved pineapple juice, vinegar, sugar, salt, and butter. Cook over hot, not boiling, water for 12 minutes or until mixture thickens, stirring constantly. Remove from heat and cool. Combine well-drained oranges, pineapple, white cherries, marshmallows, and maraschino cherries; add cooled cooked mixture. Mix gently; fold in whipped cream. Pour into a serving bowl, cover, and refrigerate for 24 hours. Yield: 8 servings.

When Grilling Chicken

For outdoor grilling, place bony or rib-cage side of chicken down next to heat first. The bones act as an insulator and prevent chicken from browning too fast.

Chicken Breast Dinner From the Grill

Dinner for Four

Barbecued Chicken Breasts

Deluxe Broccoli with Shrimp Sauce

Sliced Tomatoes

Sour Cream-Dill Potato Salad

Walnut-Butterscotch Pie

Barbecued Chicken Breasts

2 chicken breasts, cut into halves
1 clove garlic, crushed
¼ cup olive oil
½ teaspoon thyme
½ teaspoon dry mustard
¼ cup wine vinegar

Clean and wash chicken breasts; set aside. Combine crushed garlic, olive oil, thyme, mustard, and vinegar to make a basting sauce. Place chicken breasts on grill over medium heat. Cook about 10 minutes on each side before beginning to baste with sauce. Continue cooking, basting, and turning chicken until done, about 30 minutes. Yield: 4 servings.

Deluxe Broccoli with Shrimp Sauce

2 (10-ounce) packages
**   frozen broccoli spears**
¼ cup chive cream cheese
¼ cup milk
1 (10½-ounce) can condensed
**   cream of shrimp soup**
2 tablespoons freshly squeezed
**   lemon juice**
2 tablespoons toasted
**   slivered almonds**

Cook broccoli according to package directions. Drain and set aside. Blend cream cheese and milk in small saucepan; add soup and mix well. Cook and stir until mixture is hot. Add lemon juice and mix well. Spread broccoli in an 11- x 8- x 2-inch dish. Pour sauce over broccoli and sprinkle with almonds. Bake at 350° about 10 minutes, or until mixture is bubbly. Yield: 6 to 8 servings.

Need a Flat Plate?

A cookie sheet placed on top of the grill makes an acceptable flat plate.

Sour Cream-Dill Potato Salad

4 cups cooked, diced potatoes
¼ cup olive oil
1 cup diced celery
1 small purple onion, grated
3 tablespoons wine vinegar

1 teaspoon salt
¼ teaspoon black pepper
½ teaspoon dry dill weed
¾ to 1 cup commercial
    sour cream

Combine potatoes and olive oil while potatoes are still warm. Combine other ingredients in a small bowl; pour over potatoes and toss gently. Cover and refrigerate several hours for flavors to blend. Yield: 6 servings.

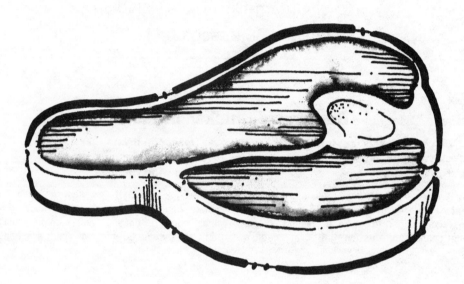

Walnut-Butterscotch Pie

3 eggs
1 cup dark corn syrup
⅔ cup sugar
1 tablespoon margarine, melted
¼ teaspoon salt

1 teaspoon vanilla extract or 3
    tablespoons bourbon
1½ cups chopped walnuts
1 (10- or 11-inch) unbaked pastry
    shell

Beat eggs slightly; add corn syrup, sugar, margarine, salt, vanilla or bourbon, and chopped walnuts. Spoon mixture into prepared pastry shell and bake at 450° for about 8 minutes; reduce heat to 350° and bake an additional 30 minutes, or until filling is set. Insert a knife in center of filling; if blade comes out clean, pie is done. Yield: 1 (10- or 11-inch) pie.

Tip for a Perfect Pie Shell

When baking an empty pie shell, prick it thoroughly along the bottom with a fork. Cut a piece of aluminum foil to fit bottom of shell, place it in pan, and fill pan with dried beans or rice to prevent pie crust from bubbling.

Barbecued Pork Loin

Dinner for Six to Eight

Sangría Southern
Barbecued Pork Loin
Creamy Eggplant Custard
Hot Potato Salad
Blueberry Coupe

Sangría Southern

1 lemon, thinly sliced
1 orange, thinly sliced
1 lime, thinly sliced
1 to 2 tablespoons sugar
1 jigger Triple Sec or
orange liqueur

1 (4/5 quart) bottle dry
red wine
½ cup chilled club soda

Remove seeds from sliced lemon, orange, and lime; place slices in glass pitcher and add sugar to taste. Do not add too much sugar until after wine has been added. Allow to stand a few minutes; add Triple Sec and stir with wooden spoon, bruising fruit to extract juices. Add wine and chill until time to serve.

Add ice cubes and chilled club soda to pitcher. Serve in punch cups with an ice cube and some fruit slices in each. Yield: about 12 servings.

Barbecued Pork Loin

1 (5- to 8-pound) pork loin
2 (18-ounce) cans pineapple juice
½ cup Worcestershire sauce
¼ cup soy sauce

1 teaspoon hot sauce
1 cup cooked, pitted prunes
Ice cream salt
1 tablespoon black peppercorns

Have butcher remove shin bone and tie roast at 3- to 4-inch intervals. Slash pork fat in several places in diamond shape.

Combine pineapple juice, Worcestershire, soy sauce, and hot sauce. Place roast in an enameled pan and put prunes around roast. Pour marinade mixture over all, and let marinate overnight in refrigerator.

The next day, remove roast from pan, reserving marinade. Pierce loin from both ends with spit of rotisserie. Stuff slashes of roast with prunes. Rub ice cream salt onto roast, and press peppercorns into meat.

Place rotisserie on grill over low heat. Baste often, as meat cooks. Cook until meat reaches desired degree of doneness. Remove from spit and place on wooden platter; pour 1 cup of marinade over loin, and allow to rest 5 minutes. Carve and serve. Yield: 6 to 8 servings.

Creamy Eggplant Custard

1 large eggplant (approximately
  1½ pounds)
  Salted water
4 eggs, beaten
1 cup half-and-half
¼ cup butter or margarine, melted

½ teaspoon salt
¼ teaspoon black pepper
⅛ teaspoon dill weed
¼ cup finely chopped
  fresh parsley

Peel eggplant and cut into ¼-inch cubes. Heat about 2½ cups salted water in a 4-quart saucepan; add eggplant and cook until fully tender. Stir occasionally, and cook for about 8 minutes. Remove from water and drain well.

Put eggplant into a large bowl and mash until very smooth. You should have about 2 cups mashed eggplant. Add the beaten eggs, half-and-half, butter or margarine, salt, pepper, dill weed, and chopped parsley. Beat mixture until light and fluffy. Pour mixture into a greased, shallow 1½-quart baking dish that can be taken to barbecue table. Bake, uncovered, at 325° for about 35 minutes, or until mixture is set when knife inserted in center comes out clean. Serve hot. Yield: 6 to 8 servings.

Hot Potato Salad

6 medium potatoes (about
  2 pounds)
8 slices bacon
¼ cup bacon drippings
1½ tablespoons all-purpose flour
1 cup water
⅓ cup vinegar
1 teaspoon salt

⅛ teaspoon black pepper
1 tablespoon sugar
2 stalks celery, sliced
1 small head romaine lettuce,
  broken into bite-size pieces
1 pared cucumber, sliced
2 small onions, sliced
6 radishes, sliced

This is best cooked in an electric skillet close by the barbecue table, since it is served directly from the pan it is cooked in. It can be cooking while loin is on the rotisserie.

Cook potatoes in salted water in an electric skillet; cool, slice, and set aside. Cook bacon until crumbly; drain on paper towels, crumble and set aside. Measure ¼ cup bacon drippings; add flour, water, vinegar, salt, pepper, and sugar. Stir well, and cook slowly until mixture thickens.

When sauce thickens, add layer of potatoes, celery, romaine, cucumber, and onion; repeat layers until all has been used. Toss gently. Top with crumbled bacon and sliced radishes. Serve hot. Yield: 6 to 8 servings.

Blueberry Coupe

1½ cups port wine
½ cup brown sugar
3 tablespoons cornstarch
¾ teaspoon grated lemon rind

¾ cup blueberries, fresh
  or frozen
6 to 8 scoops vanilla ice cream

The sauce for this dessert can be made in advance and kept warm. Spoon ice cream into serving dishes and keep in freezer until ready to serve.

Combine wine, brown sugar, cornstarch, and lemon rind in saucepan. Heat until sugar dissolves; add blueberries and continue heating until blueberries are warm through. Spoon sauce over ice cream and serve. Yield: 6 to 8 servings.

Beachcomber Party

Dinner for Eight to Ten

Hawaiian Grilled Spareribs
Blender Potato Casserole
Cold Vegetable Platter
Curried Compote
Ginger Pick-Up

Hawaiian Grilled Spareribs

4 racks of spareribs
  Garlic salt to taste
  Pepper to taste
4 cups orange juice
1 cup Champale

½ cup brown sugar, firmly packed
½ cup soy sauce
4 tablespoons instant
  minced onion

Sprinkle ribs with garlic salt and pepper. Put ribs in shallow glass or enameled pan. Combine orange juice, Champale, brown sugar, soy sauce, and onion; pour over ribs. Marinate for 1 to 2 hours. Drain ribs; save marinade. Grill ribs on rack about 6 inches above hot coals. Cook 15 to 20 minutes on one side; turn ribs and cook 15 to 20 minutes longer. Brush with marinade every few minutes. Continue to cook ribs until done. Cut into serving pieces. Yield: 10 servings.

Blender Potato Casserole

1 cup milk
3 eggs
1 teaspoon salt
¼ teaspoon pepper
2 tablespoons butter
  or margarine

1 cup cubed Cheddar cheese
½ green pepper, diced
1 small onion, quartered
4 medium uncooked potatoes,
  peeled and cubed

Combine all ingredients in a blender container in the order listed; cover and blend on high speed just until potatoes go through the blades (do not overblend). Pour the mixture into a greased 1½-quart casserole dish, and bake uncovered at 350° for 50 minutes to 1 hour. Yield: 8 to 10 servings.

Precook Spareribs

Precooking spareribs in the kitchen cuts down on cooking time on the grill. Boiling in a small amount of water, or baking at 350° helps to remove some of the fat and eliminates "flare-ups" on the grill. Drain well before putting on grill, and brush on marinade as ribs cook.

Cold Vegetable Platter

1 quart salad greens
2 carrots, sliced
1 cucumber, sliced
2 small red onions, sliced
½ head cauliflower, cut into flowerets

⅛ pound mushrooms, trimmed and sliced
1 cup sliced radishes
1½ cups sliced celery
2 tomatoes, cut into wedges
Beer Dressing

Wash salad greens and tear into bite-size pieces. Fill salad bowl with greens. Arrange vegetables in layers starting with carrots and continuing with remainder of vegetables. Serve with Beer Dressing. Yield: 10 servings.

Beer Dressing

¾ cup salad oil
½ cup beer
1½ teaspoons Worcestershire sauce
1 (10½-ounce) can tomato soup

½ small onion, minced
½ clove garlic, crushed
1½ teaspoons sugar
1 teaspoon salt
1½ teaspoons prepared horseradish

Put all ingredients in blender and blend until smooth. Chill until ready to serve. (It may be necessary to whirl in blender again before serving.) Yield: 3½ cups.

Curried Compote

1 (16-ounce) can apricot halves, drained
1 (16-ounce) can purple plums, drained
1 (16-ounce) can peach halves, drained
3 or 4 thin orange slices, cut into halves

½ cup orange juice or ½ cup Champale
¼ cup brown sugar
½ teaspoon freshly grated lemon peel
4 teaspoons curry powder
2 tablespoons butter, melted

Arrange drained fruit in shallow baking dish. Combine orange juice, brown sugar, lemon peel, and curry powder; mix well and pour over fruit. Drizzle butter over fruit. Put on back of grill and simmer for 15 to 20 minutes. Serve warm. Yield: 10 servings.

Ginger Pick-Up

1 cup orange-flavored instant breakfast drink
1½ cups pineapple juice

1 (1-pint 12-ounce) bottle ginger ale

Combine orange-flavored instant breakfast drink, pineapple juice, and ginger ale; stir well to dissolve. Pour over ice cubes to serve. Yield: 8 to 10 servings.

Ham-on-the-Rotisserie

Dinner for Eight

Ham with Port Wine

Peas Supreme

Grits Soufflé

Sliced Tomatoes

Shakertown Lemon Pie

Ham with Port Wine

1 (4- to 5-pound) precooked ham
1 cup port wine

½ teaspoon ground cinnamon
1 (12-ounce) can apricot nectar

Pierce ham in several places with a meat fork, and place in a glass bowl. Combine wine, cinnamon, and apricot nectar; pour over ham, and allow ham to remain in marinade for several hours, turning frequently. Remove ham from marinade and place on rotisserie. Grill over medium heat about 1 hour, basting often with marinade. Yield: 8 servings.

Peas Supreme

2 (10-ounce) packages frozen
green peas
1 (4-ounce) can mushroom
pieces, drained

1 tablespoon diced pimiento
1 tablespoon butter or
margarine, melted

Cook peas according to package directions. Sauté mushroom pieces and pimiento in melted butter for about 3 minutes; add to hot, cooked and drained peas. **Serve hot.** Yield: 8 servings.

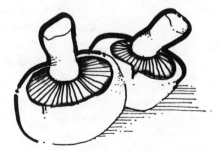

Quick Baked Potatoes

To bake potatoes in half the usual time, let them stand in boiling water for 15 minutes before baking in a very hot oven.

Grits Soufflé

5 cups cold water
1 cup uncooked regular grits
½ cup margarine, softened
2 eggs, beaten
½ teaspoon red pepper

Dash salt
Dash hot sauce
½ pound sharp Cheddar
    cheese, shredded

Bring water to a boil in large saucepan; add grits and cook until mixture thickens. Add other ingredients and mix well. Spoon mixture into a greased 2-quart casserole dish. Bake at 350° for 1 hour. This may be prepared ahead of time and refrigerated until time to bake. Yield: 8 servings.

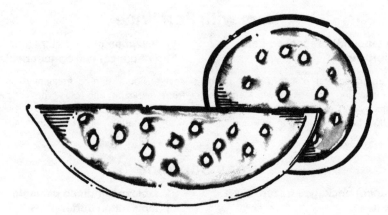

Shakertown Lemon Pie

2 lemons
2 cups sugar
4 eggs, beaten well

1 (9-inch) unbaked double
    crust pastry

Slice lemons into paper-thin slices. Remove seeds and place lemon slices in a bowl. Add sugar, stir well, and let stand for at least 2 hours. Add beaten eggs to lemon-sugar mixture and spoon into unbaked pastry shell. Roll out top crust, put top on pie, and cut slits in top for steam to escape. Bake at 450° for 15 minutes; reduce heat to 350° and bake an additional 35 minutes. Test with a silver knife; pie is done when knife inserted in center comes out clean. Yield: 1 (9-inch) pie.

Seasoning the Meat

Most meats cooked on the grill need little or no seasoning at the beginning of the cooking period. Some cooks prefer to cook the meat without sauce and serve sauce on the side. At any rate, use sauce only during the last half of cooking time.

Ham-on-the-Grill

Dinner for Six to Eight

Sour Cream Dip with Carrot and Celery Sticks

Sangría Blanca

Glazed Grilled Ham

Green Chile Hominy Casserole

Grilled Zucchini

Toasted English Muffins

Coconut Pound Cake

Sour Cream Dip

2 cups commercial sour cream
(use low-calorie if possible)
⅛ teaspoon fresh basil
⅛ teaspoon thyme
⅛ teaspoon marjoram

¼ teaspoon onion salt
½ teaspoon seasoned salt
Carrot sticks
Celery sticks

Combine sour cream, basil, thyme, marjoram, onion salt, and seasoned salt in bowl; mix well, taste, and add more seasoning if desired. Store in a covered container in refrigerator at least 6 hours before serving.

Place bowl on table; arrange carrot and celery sticks on plate for dipping into sour cream dip. Yield: 8 servings.

Sangría Blanca

1 bottle Riesling white wine
1 (6-ounce) can frozen lemonade
concentrate, thawed

1 cup club soda
Lime slices

Combine wine and lemonade concentrate; mix well. Add club soda and stir. Serve over ice cubes. Garnish with lime slices. Yield: 6 to 8 servings.

Glazed Grilled Ham

1 (3- or 4-pound) precooked
boneless ham

½ cup dark corn syrup
½ cup pineapple juice

Slice ham into ½-inch slices. Tie securely into its original shape as nearly as possible. Cook at low heat on a covered grill about 1 hour. Combine corn syrup and pineapple juice and baste ham at 15-minute intervals. Yield: 8 servings.

Green Chile Hominy Casserole

2 (16-ounce) cans hominy, drained
3 tablespoons margarine, melted
3 tablespoons all-purpose flour
1 (8-ounce) can green chiles
   (use less if desired)

Milk
1 tablespoon chopped pimiento
1½ cups shredded sharp
   Cheddar cheese

Place hominy in oblong, buttered casserole dish; set aside. Combine margarine and flour in saucepan; heat and stir until smooth. Drain juice from chiles and add enough milk to make 2 cups; add liquid to flour mixture. Continue to stir over low heat until well-blended. Add chiles and pimiento. Pour sauce over hominy; sprinkle with cheese. Bake at 350° for 30 minutes. (Chiles make this casserole very hot.) Yield: 8 servings.

Grilled Zucchini

3 tablespoons salad oil
1½ teaspoons basil

8 zucchini squash,
   sliced lengthwise

Combine salad oil and basil. Brush zucchini with marinade and allow to marinate 1 hour. Place zucchini on grill on low heat; turn frequently. Yield: 6 to 8 servings.

Toasted English Muffins

8 to 10 English muffins, split
   in halves

½ cup butter or margarine,
   softened

After all food has been removed from grill, spread softened butter on muffin halves and place on grill to toast. Serve hot. Yield: 8 servings.

Coconut Pound Cake

1 cup butter or margarine, softened
½ cup vegetable shortening
3 cups sugar
6 eggs
½ teaspoon almond extract

1 teaspoon coconut flavoring
3 cups all-purpose flour
1 cup milk
1 (3½-ounce) can flaked coconut

Cream butter, shortening, and sugar until light and fluffy. Add eggs, one at a time, beating well after each addition. Add flavorings and mix well. Alternately add flour and milk, beating after each addition. Stir in coconut. Spoon batter into a 10-inch greased tubepan or Bundt pan. Bake at 350° for 1 hour and 15 minutes. Yield: 1 (10-inch) cake.

Preventing Runovers

To keep vegetables, spaghetti, or rice from boiling over the sides of saucepan, rub butter around edge of pan.

Pork Chop Special

Dinner for Eight

Herb-Flavored Pork Chops

Cucumbers with Sour Cream

Roasted Seasoned Corn

Sliced Tomatoes

Garlic Bread

Pineapple Fluff

Herb-Flavored Pork Chops

8 (1-inch thick) loin pork chops
2 (12-ounce) cans tomato juice
1 teaspoon salt

½ teaspoon pepper
1 to 2 tablespoons basil

Put loin chops in flat container. Combine tomato juice, salt, pepper, and basil and pour over chops. Marinate several hours in refrigerator. Remove chops carefully from marinade so that basil clings to chops. Cook over low heat on grill until meat is done, basting as meat cooks. Turn chops often. Yield: 8 servings.

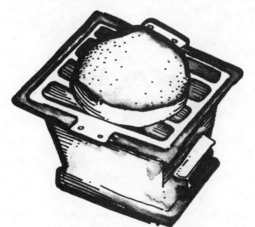

Cucumbers with Sour Cream

6 medium cucumbers
3 teaspoons salt
¼ teaspoon black pepper
6 tablespoons minced chives

2 cups commercial sour cream
4 tablespoons freshly squeezed lemon juice

Pare and slice cucumbers. Combine other ingredients and pour over cucumbers. Cover dish and let stand in refrigerator for several hours before serving. Yield: 8 to 10 servings.

Roasted Seasoned Corn

8 ears corn, fresh or frozen
½ cup butter or
   margarine, melted
1 tablespoon minced parsley

Dash paprika
1 teaspoon salt
Dash fresh ground pepper

Remove husks and silks from fresh corn, or thaw frozen ears. Combine melted butter, parsley, paprika, salt, and black pepper and spread liberally over each ear of corn. Wrap each ear of corn in a square of heavy-duty aluminum foil. Bake on grill for about 15 to 20 minutes, turning two or three times. Serve hot directly from foil. Yield: 8 servings.

Garlic Bread

(page 82)

Pineapple Fluff

1 fresh pineapple
¼ cup sugar
2 cups miniature marshmallows

½ pint whipping cream, whipped
Sliced maraschino cherries

Pare and cut pineapple into small pieces. Place a layer in a bowl, sprinkle with sugar and marshmallows; continue until all has been placed in bowl. Cover bowl and let stand for several hours. To serve, fold in whipped cream and spoon into serving dishes. Garnish with cherries. Yield: 8 servings.

Balance Meat on Rotisserie

If you are using the rotisserie with your barbecue grill, be sure that the rotisserie rod is inserted in the center of the meat, lengthwise, and the spit forks tightened so that meat will be well-balanced and rotisserie will turn evenly. Then insert meat thermometer so that it reaches the center of the meat, being careful that it does not touch a bone or the rod itself. Large cuts of meat are successfully cooked on the rotisserie.

Polynesian-on-Your-Grill

Dinner for Four to Six

Artichoke Appetizer with Lemon Sauce
Hickory-Smoked Peppered Pork Chops
Hot Applesauce
Almond Rice
Pineapple Paradise

Artichoke Appetizer with Lemon Sauce

4 to 6 artichokes
3 cloves
4 slices lemon
⅓ cup butter or margarine

½ teaspoon salt
½ teaspoon black pepper
¼ cup freshly squeezed
 lemon juice

Wash artichokes (allow one per person) in cold water. Place artichokes in boiling salted water to which garlic and lemon slices have been added. Cover and simmer for 25 to 30 minutes, or until leaves can be removed easily. Drain.

Combine butter, salt, pepper, and lemon juice in a saucepan. Heat about 1 minute. Serve with hot artichokes. Yield: 4 to 6 servings.

Note: To eat, tear off one leaf at a time, dunk in sauce, turn leaf upside-down, bite and peel. Disregard center of fuzzy choke and use a fork for eating the heart.

Hickory-Smoked Peppered Pork Chops

Buy a center cut pork loin, allowing ¾-to 1-pound per person. Have the butcher slice the loin into ¾- to 1-inch thick chop portions. Bring the pork to room temperature and cover with packaged, coarsely ground lemon-pepper marinade, 1 tablespoon per chop. Let stand while preparing fire.

For charcoal grill: Soak hickory chips in water for about 20 minutes. Using about 15 charcoal briquettes, light with a match; arrange briquettes to cover bottom of grill evenly. Put a few of the hickory chips on after fire has burned down some. Place meat on grill, and close hood if the grill has one; if it does not have a lid, cover with a new garbage can lid. Add more soaked chips if needed. Cook until meat is white inside, about 45 minutes to 1 hour.

For gas grill: Turn gas on high and light; turn heat to medium. Place dampened hickory chips onto ceramic briquettes. Put chops on grill and close lid. Cook about 45 minutes to 1 hour, turning chops once. For the most accurate guide, use a meat thermometer; it should register 190° when meat is done.

If you have become over-zealous on the quantity prepared, leftovers can be frozen. Wrap securely in heavy-duty aluminum foil, label, and freeze immediately.

Hot Applesauce

2 cups applesauce
½-inch stick cinnamon

1 whole clove
1 tablespoon prepared horseradish

Combine all ingredients in saucepan; heat quickly and serve hot. If your menu lacks color, add 2 drops of red food coloring. Yield: 4 to 6 servings.

Almond Rice

2 tablespoons salad oil
1 small onion, chopped
½ green pepper, chopped
¼ teaspoon garlic salt
¼ teaspoon black pepper

2 cups cooked rice
2 teaspoons soy sauce
½ cup slivered
   blanched almonds

Heat oil in heavy skillet. Add onion, pepper, garlic salt, and black pepper; sauté about 5 minutes over medium heat. Add rice, soy sauce, and almonds; mix well. Cook about 10 minutes, or until mixture is thoroughly heated. Yield: 4 servings.

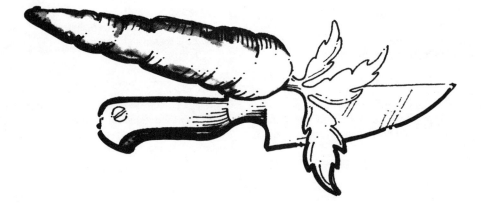

Pineapple Paradise

1 medium fresh pineapple
½ cup honey

1 tablespoon plus 1 teaspoon
   brandy (optional)

Cut pineapple into eight lengthwise wedges. Place each wedge on a double thickness of heavy-duty aluminum foil. Pour 1 tablespoon honey over each wedge. One-half teaspoon brandy may be poured over each wedge. Wrap securely in foil and place on grill set at medium setting. Cook about 20 minutes on gas or electric grill, or 15 minutes on charcoal briquettes. Yield: 8 servings.

Utensils for the Outdoor Chef

Handy outdoor utensils: Large salt and pepper shakers, roll of heavy-duty aluminum foil, asbestos mitts or potholders, long-handled fork and tongs, paintbrush for basting, and a meat thermometer for checking doneness of large pieces of meat.

Luau Spareribs

Dinner for Four to Six

Luau Spareribs

Hawaiian-Style Baked Beans

Sweet Potato Casserole

Crisp Relish

Fresh Fruit with Poppy Seed Dressing

Lime Sparkle

Luau Spareribs

2 (4½-ounce) jars strained
  peaches (baby food)
⅓ cup catsup
⅓ cup vinegar
2 tablespoons soy sauce
½ cup brown sugar

1 clove garlic, minced
2 teaspoons ground ginger
1 teaspoon salt
  Dash pepper
4 pounds meaty spareribs
  Salt and pepper

Mix all ingredients except ribs for sauce. Heat well over medium heat. Rub ribs with salt and pepper. Place bone-side down on grill over low heat. Grill about 20 minutes; turn meat-side down and grill until browned, about 10 minutes. Turn meat-side up again and brush with sauce and grill without turning, about 30 minutes, or until meat is well-done. Brush frequently with sauce. Yield: 4 to 6 servings.

Hawaiian-Style Baked Beans

2 (1-pound) cans pork and beans
¼ pound cooked ham, diced
½ teaspoon dry mustard
¼ cup brown sugar, firmly packed

2 tablespoons finely chopped onion
1 cup drained pineapple chunks
¼ cup pineapple juice

Grease a 1½-quart baking dish. Spoon a can of pork and beans in bottom of dish. Combine ham, mustard, brown sugar, onion, pineapple, and pineapple juice; spoon over layer of beans, and top with the other can of pork and beans. Cover and bake at 350° for 1 hour. Yield: 5 to 6 servings.

Allow Enough Meat

For the average appetite allow: ¼ to ½ pound ground meat per person; ⅓ to ½ pound of meat, if boneless; ¾ to 1 pound of meat, bone in, depending on size of bone; and ¼ of a chicken per person. For hearty appetites, allow more.

Sweet Potato Casserole

½ cup brown sugar, divided
⅔ cup orange juice, divided
⅓ cup margarine,
  melted and divided
2 (1-pound) cans sweet
  potatoes, drained

2 eggs
1 teaspoon salt
¼ teaspoon cloves
1 teaspoon ground cinnamon
1 cup pecans, chopped

Combine ¼ cup brown sugar, 2 teaspoons orange juice, and 2 teaspoons butter; mix and set aside to use for glaze topping. Whip potatoes until smooth; beat in eggs. Add remaining sugar, orange juice, and butter. Add salt, cloves, and cinnamon; mix well and pour into a 1½-quart casserole dish. Sprinkle pecans on top. Pour glaze topping over pecans. Bake at 350° for 40 minutes. Yield: 6 servings.

Crisp Relish

(page 45)

Fresh Fruit with Poppy Seed Dressing

(page 93)

Lime Sparkle

2 (6-ounce) cans frozen lime
  juice concentrate
Soda water

Watermelon juice
Small wedges of peeled watermelon
Orange slices

Reconstitute limeade juice concentrate according to directions on can, substituting soda water for tap water. Sweeten with a little watermelon juice (a piece of watermelon on a pieplate is easily "juiced" with a potato masher—then strain). A small wedge of peeled watermelon in the drink and an orange slice on each glass completes the picture. Yield: 6 servings.

Note: Watermelon juice is extremely sweet, so add it sparingly until sweet enough to suit your own family.

Let Ice Do a Cool Job for You

If you want ice that is not clouded or honeycombed with air pockets, use distilled water. Syphon into refrigerator molds by holding syphon tube against bottom of mold and pour slowly. If you do not have distilled water handy, use water that has been boiled and cooled slightly.

Soy Sauced Pork Chops

Dinner for Six

Barbecued Soy Sauced Pork Chops

Zucchini Casserole

Pan Browned Rice

Shredded Lettuce with Vinegar and Oil Dressing

Crusty Commercial French Bread

Raspberry Dream

Barbecued Soy Sauced Pork Chops

½ cup soy sauce
1 clove garlic, crushed
Dash pepper

6 (1-inch thick) pork chops
Barbecue sauce

Combine soy sauce, garlic, and pepper; marinate pork chops in glass bowl for 1 hour in marinade, turning every 15 minutes. Drain. Grill 30 minutes on each side, basting often with your favorite barbecue sauce. Yield: 6 servings.

Zucchini Casserole

8 small zucchini squash,
   sliced lengthwise
2 tomatoes, cut into eighths
½ green pepper, cut into
   thin strips
¾ cup chopped onion

½ teaspoon salt
½ teaspoon Beau Monde seasoning
¼ teaspoon pepper
¼ cup grated Parmesan cheese
½ teaspoon sugar
¼ cup butter, melted

Place zucchini slices in buttered, oblong casserole dish. Place tomatoes, green pepper, and onion between zucchini slices. Sprinkle salt, seasoning, pepper, cheese, and sugar on top. Drizzle butter evenly over top. Bake, uncovered, at 350° for 45 minutes to 1 hour. Yield: 6 servings.

Don't Serve Cloudy Tea

Make your tea ahead of time, but do not put it in the refrigerator or it will turn cloudy. In making tea to be served on ice, use 50 percent more tea to allow for melting ice. Let steeped tea cool to room temperature, then pour over ice cubes.

Pan Browned Rice

1 small onion, chopped
½ medium green pepper
¼ cup butter or margarine
1½ cups regular rice, uncooked
2 (10½-ounce) cans beef broth

1 (8¼-ounce) can pineapple
   tidbits, drained
1 tablespoon soy sauce
½ teaspoon ground allspice

Sauté onion and green pepper in melted butter or margarine until both are limp but not browned. Stir in rice and sauté until rice turns yellow. Stir in other ingredients; cover skillet and cook until rice is tender and all liquid has been absorbed. Yield: 6 servings.

Raspberry Dream

1 envelope unflavored gelatin
¼ cup cold water
1 (8-ounce) package cream
   cheese, softened
½ cup sugar

½ teaspoon almond extract
   Dash salt
1 cup milk
½ pint whipping cream, whipped
   Raspberry Sauce

Soften gelatin in water and heat until dissolved; set aside. Combine cream cheese, sugar, almond extract, and salt; blend until smooth. Gradually add milk and gelatin; fold in whipped cream. Pour into eight small molds or a 1-quart mold. Refrigerate until set. (This can be frozen and thawed when ready to use.) Yield: 8 servings.

Raspberry Sauce

1 (10-ounce) package
   frozen raspberries

1 tablespoon cornstarch
2 tablespoons sherry

Thaw and drain raspberries. Combine raspberry syrup, cornstarch, and sherry; cook over low heat until thick. Add raspberries; blend well. Refrigerate and serve over molds. Yield: 1 cup.

Containers for Marinating Meats

Glass or enameled dishes are preferred for marinating meats. Marinades containing soy sauce should always be put in enamel or glass; other marinades may be put in plastic containers.

Glazed Pork Loin Special

Dinner for Six to Eight

Glazed Pork Loin

Baked Cheese Grits

Broccoli with Shrimp Sauce

Special Cole Slaw

Bacon-Onion French Bread

Watermelon Boat

Glazed Pork Loin

1 (6- to 8-pound) pork loin
Salt and pepper
¼ cup soy sauce
¼ cup freshly squeezed lemon juice
2 tablespoons sugar

1 teaspoon dry mustard
¼ teaspoon ground cloves
1 teaspoon ground ginger
2 tablespoons commercial steak sauce

Salt and pepper loin; put on rotisserie over low heat for 1 hour. Combine all other ingredients; heat to boiling point. Brush sauce on loin and continue to cook for at least another hour (or longer depending on size of loin). Continue to baste with sauce. Yield: 6 to 8 servings.

Baked Cheese Grits

1½ cups regular grits
6 cups boiling salted water
½ cup butter or margarine
1 (6-ounce) roll garlic cheese
3 tablespoons cooking sherry

3 tablespoons Worcestershire sauce
½ teaspoon hot sauce
3 eggs, beaten

Cook grits in boiling salted water about 2 or 3 minutes. Blend in butter or margarine, cheese, sherry, and sauces; stir in beaten eggs and mix well. Spoon mixture into a 2-quart baking dish and bake at 300° about 1 hour. Serve hot. Yield: 6 to 8 servings.

Is the Grill Ready?

Allow about 30 minutes for charcoal briquettes to turn ash-gray before putting food on grill. To make fire building easier, carry charcoal briquettes in milk cartons, and burn cartons and briquettes together. When using gas or electric heat, preheat the grill.

Broccoli with Shrimp Sauce

2 (10-ounce) packages
  frozen broccoli
1 (10½-ounce) can undiluted
  cream of shrimp soup

½ cup diced almonds

Cook broccoli according to package directions. Drain and place in a 1½-quart casserole dish. Spoon shrimp soup over broccoli, and sprinkle almonds on top. Bake at 300° for about 15 minutes. Yield: 6 to 8 servings.

Special Cole Slaw

1 medium head cabbage,
  chopped fine
1 (8¼-ounce) can pineapple tidbits,
  drained
2 carrots, chopped fine
1 small green pepper, diced
1 large apple, unpeeled and
  chopped fine

½ cup flaked coconut
½ cup miniature marshmallows
7 tablespoons evaporated milk
7 tablespoons sugar
7 tablespoons vinegar
½ teaspoon celery salt
½ teaspoon onion salt

Combine first seven ingredients in large bowl. Put evaporated milk, sugar, vinegar, celery, and onion salt in a jar and shake well to make dressing. Add to cabbage mixture and toss. Cover bowl and chill until time to serve. Yield: 6 to 8 servings.

Bacon-Onion French Bread

1 (1-pound) loaf
  French bread
½ (1⅜-ounce) package dry onion
  soup mix

6 or 8 slices crisp
  bacon, crumbled
½ cup butter or margarine

Slice bread in 1-inch slices almost through loaf. Combine soup mix, crumbled bacon, and butter or margarine. Melt and mix well. Spread on slices. Wrap loaf in aluminum foil and heat on grill. Yield: 6 to 8 servings.

Watermelon Boat

Select a nicely shaped oval watermelon and remove top third lengthwise. Use a melon ball cutter and scoop out nice little balls from the large portion. Chill. Combine melon balls with chunks of fresh pineapple, green grapes, cantaloupe balls, and peach slices, if desired. Put fruit into melon boat, garnish with mint leaves, and cover with plastic wrap. Chill until ready to serve.

Meat Roasting Tip

Slow, even heat is the key to successful roasting of meat. The meat will not be charred and will cook evenly and shrink less.

Southern Spareribs Specialty

Dinner for Four

Barbecued Spareribs

Sauerkraut in Wine

Grilled or Boiled Corn-on-the-Cob

Garlic Bread

Buttermilk Sherbet

Barbecued Spareribs

1 cup catsup
½ cup dark corn syrup
½ cup cider vinegar
¼ cup Worcestershire sauce
¼ cup Dijon mustard

1 to 2 tablespoons chili powder
2 teaspoons salt
¼ teaspoon hot sauce
**4 pounds spareribs, cut in 1
  or 2 rib pieces**

Blend catsup, corn syrup, vinegar, Worcestershire sauce, mustard, chili powder, salt, and hot sauce; set aside. Tear off four sheets of 18-inch-wide heavy-duty aluminum foil. Each sheet should be 22 inches long. Place two sheets together to make two double 18- x 22-inch sheets.

Arrange half the spareribs on double sheet so that there are no more than two layers deep. Lift up edges of foil slightly and pour half the sauce over ribs. Close package by using a double fold down center and at ends.

Repeat packaging for second half of ribs. Place on grill over very low heat and cook for about 1 hour. Cut packages open with a knife or scissors. Yield: 4 servings.

Sauerkraut in Wine

1 (27-ounce) can sauerkraut, drained
2 cloves garlic, crushed

1 teaspoon freshly ground pepper
2 cups dry white wine

Combine sauerkraut with crushed garlic, black pepper, and wine in a 2-quart casserole dish or in an electric skillet. Cover and simmer for 30 to 45 minutes. Add more wine if necessary. Serve hot. Yield: 4 servings.

For a Browner Barbecue

Add more catsup or tomato paste to your barbecue sauce during the last stages of cooking for a browner, crustier piece of meat.

Grilled Corn-on-the-Cob

4 to 6 ears corn
Softened butter

Salt and pepper

Get young tender corn as fresh from the field as possible. You may want to cook two ears per person, or at least two for the heartiest eaters.

Remove large outer husks from young tender corn; turn back inner husks and remove silk. Spread corn generously with softened butter.

Pull husks back over ears, and tie with a heavy twine. Some cooks dip ears of corn in cold water at this point. Roast on grill for about 10 to 20 minutes, turning frequently. Serve at once with salt, pepper, and additional softened butter. Yield: 4 to 6 servings.

Boiled Corn-on-the-Cob

4 to 6 ears fresh sweet corn
Boiling water

Butter or margarine

Remove husks from fresh young ears of corn. Put into a large saucepan and cover with boiling water. Boil for 8 to 10 minutes, depending on size

of ears. Remove from water, drain, and serve hot with butter or margarine. Yield: 4 to 6 servings.

Garlic Bread

½ cup butter or margarine
1 clove garlic, crushed

1 (1-pound) loaf French bread

Melt butter or margarine, and stir in crushed garlic. Slice bread and spread each slice with butter. Wrap the loaf in aluminum foil and

place on the back of the grill. Turn the loaf often; serve hot. Yield: 4 servings.

Buttermilk Sherbet

2 cups fresh buttermilk
¾ cup sugar
1 (8¼-ounce) can crushed
   pineapple, undrained
   Grated rind of 1 lemon

2 to 3 tablespoons freshly
   squeezed lemon juice
   Few drops green food coloring
2 envelopes unflavored gelatin
2 tablespoons cold water
1 egg white, stiffly beaten

Combine buttermilk, sugar, pineapple and juice, rind and juice of lemon, and food coloring. Soften gelatin in cold water; dissolve over boiling water and add to buttermilk mixture. Pour into refrigerator trays and freeze until firm.

Remove trays from freezer and put mixture

in large bowl. Break mixture with a fork, then beat until light and fluffy. Fold in egg white; return to refrigerator trays and freeze until firm. This mixture may be frozen in a half-gallon electric or hand-turned ice cream freezer. Yield: 4 to 6 servings.

Saucy Sparerib Dinner

Dinner for Four

Saucy Barbecued Spareribs

Corn Pudding

Grilled Tomatoes

Savory Green Bean Salad

Grilled Cinnamon Apples

Saucy Barbecued Spareribs

1 tablespoon celery seed
1 tablespoon chili powder
½ cup brown sugar
2 teaspoons salt
1 teaspoon paprika
2½ pounds meaty spareribs
1 (8-ounce) can tomato sauce
¼ cup vinegar

Combine celery seed, chili powder, sugar, salt, and paprika. Rub a third of the mixture on ribs. Add tomato sauce and vinegar to remaining mixture. Cook ribs over low heat about 1 hour, basting occasionally with the sauce. Yield: 4 servings.

Corn Pudding

2 tablespoons butter
2 tablespoons salad oil
½ medium onion, chopped fine
1 cup whole-kernel corn,
    canned or fresh
1 tablespoon sugar
    Salt and pepper to taste
3 egg yolks, well beaten
½ cup shredded Cheddar cheese
3 egg whites, stiffly beaten

Heat butter and salad oil in skillet. Sauté onion; add corn, sugar, salt, and pepper. Cool and stir in egg yolks and shredded cheese. Fold in stiffly beaten egg whites. Spoon into a well-greased 11- x 8-inch baking dish and set in a pan of water. Bake uncovered at 350° for 1 hour. Yield: 4 servings.

Cut the Spattering

To keep oil or shortening from spattering when you are frying foods, sprinkle in a little salt.

Grilled Tomatoes

15 cherry tomatoes
2 tablespoons butter, melted
2 teaspoons sweet basil

2 teaspoons chopped parsley
Salt to taste
Cracked pepper to taste

Place tomatoes on a large piece of heavy-duty aluminum foil. Combine butter, basil, parsley, salt, and pepper; pour this mixture over tomatoes. Wrap foil tightly and cook over medium heat on grill for about 15 minutes. Yield: 3 to 4 servings.

Savory Green Bean Salad

1 (16-ounce) can green
  beans, drained
6 tablespoons salad oil
3 tablespoons vinegar
½ teaspoon salt
½ teaspoon pepper
1 onion, minced

4 hard-cooked eggs, chopped
2 teaspoons vinegar
3 tablespoons mayonnaise
1 teaspoon prepared mustard
4 strips bacon, fried crisp
  and crumbled
Lettuce

Combine beans, salad oil, 3 tablespoons vinegar, salt, pepper, and onion; mix well. Cover and chill. Combine eggs, 2 teaspoons vinegar, mayonnaise, and mustard; mix well. Cover and chill. When ready to serve, toss bacon lightly with beans. Heap in lettuce-lined bowl and top with egg mixture. Yield: 4 to 6 servings.

Grilled Cinnamon Apples

4 apples
4 tablespoons red-hot
  cinnamon candy

4 tablespoons raisins
Butter

Core apples and place on heavy-duty aluminum foil. Fill hole of each apple with 1 tablespoon of cinnamon candy and 1 tablespoon of raisins. Dot with butter. Bring foil up loosely over apples and twist ends together to seal. Cook over glowing coals for 30 minutes or until done. Yield: 4 servings.

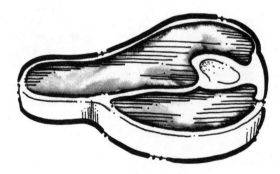

Bacon Delight

For a new bacon treat, dip bacon slices in beaten eggs, then in crushed cracker crumbs and broil.

Frankfurter Special

Dinner for Six to Eight

Cucumber Soup

Barbecued Frankfurters

Foiled French Fries

Sliced Tomatoes and Lettuce Wedges

Quick Brownies

Cucumber Soup

1 quart buttermilk
1 large cucumber, diced
½ teaspoon ground cinnamon
    or allspice

Salt to taste
4 or 5 leaves of mint, crushed

Combine all ingredients and put in covered container in refrigerator to chill at least 2 or 3 hours. Yield: 1 quart.

Barbecued Frankfurters

1 large onion, chopped
2 cloves garlic, minced
1⅓ cups catsup
2 teaspoons chili powder
1 tablespoon dry mustard
1 teaspoon salt

¼ cup red wine vinegar
1 cup water
1 (1-pound) package frankfurters
1 (8-ounce) package elbow
    spaghetti, cooked

Combine onion, garlic, catsup, chili powder, mustard, salt, vinegar, and water; bring to a boil. Cover and simmer for 25 minutes. Grill frankfurters over hot coals; brown evenly. Cut into bite-size pieces. Add to barbecue sauce mixture. Arrange cooked spaghetti on platter; pour frankfurter mixture over top. Yield: 6 to 8 servings.

Use Your Corn Popper

Wieners may be cooked in a corn popper over the grill if you do not have a hinged rack or individual skewers. Give them a hearty shake occasionally so they will cook evenly.

Foiled French Fries

**1½ pounds frozen French-
fried potatoes**

**½ cup grated Parmesan cheese
1 teaspoon salt**

Thaw potatoes slightly. Divide into six equal portions and put on individual squares of heavy-duty aluminum foil. Combine Parmesan cheese and salt and sprinkle **over potat**oes. Seal packets and place on grill. Cook over low heat about 15 minutes, turning packets occasionally. Yield: 6 servings.

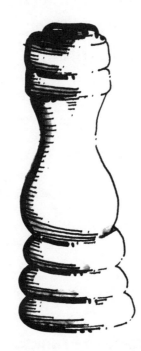

Quick Brownies

**1 (22½-ounce) package fudge
brownie mix**

**1 (12-ounce) package quick fudge mix
1 cup miniature marshmallows**

Prepare brownies according to directions on package. Bake in a greased 13- x 9- x 2-inch baking pan. After brownies have baked 15 minutes, prepare fudge mix according to package directions. When brownies are done, remove from oven and sprinkle with marshmallows. Spread hot fudge over top of marshmallows, and allow to cool thoroughly before cutting into bars. Yield: 24 bar cookies.

Controlling the Heat

You do not need an inferno to barbecue. The most common mistake made is the use of heat that is too high. This results in cremating instead of barbecuing the meat. Place meat about 4 to 5 inches above the heat unless instructions state otherwise. Just before pieces of meat are completely done, move to outer edge of grill where they'll finish cooking and stay hot but won't cook as rapidly as when left in center of grill.

Teen Tempter Party
Party for Six

Batter-Up Corndogs

French-Fried Onions

Cheddar Deviled Eggs

Cheesy Vegetable Salad

Colonial Apple Pie

Tangy Punch

Batter-Up Corndogs

½ **cup cornmeal**
½ **cup all-purpose flour**
1 **teaspoon salt**
½ **teaspoon pepper**
1 **egg, beaten**

½ **cup milk**
2 **tablespoons salad oil**
12 **frankfurters**
  Salad oil for frying

Sift dry ingredients together; add egg, milk, and 2 tablespoons salad oil. Beat until smooth. Dip frankfurters into batter; drain. Fry in deep oil heated to 375° for 2 to 3 minutes or until golden brown. Yield: 1 dozen corndogs.

French-Fried Onions

4 **large white onions, peeled**
1 **cup milk**
2 **eggs, beaten**

2 **cups self-rising flour**
  Salad oil for frying
  Salt

Cut peeled onions into ¼-inch slices and separate into rings. Combine milk and eggs; soak rings in milk-egg mixture for 2 hours. Drain. Dredge rings in flour and dip again in milk-egg mixture. Dredge rings in flour again and fry in deep oil heated to 365° until golden brown. Drain on absorbent paper. Salt and serve immediately. Yield: 6 servings.

Cheddar Deviled Eggs

6 **hard-cooked eggs**
2 **tablespoons shredded**
  Cheddar cheese

1 **tablespoon mayonnaise**
1 **tablespoon prepared mustard**

Peel eggs and cut in half. Put yolks into small bowl and mash with a fork. Add cheese, mayonnaise, and mustard; mix well. Refill eggs with yolk mixture. Yield: 12 halves.

Cheesy Vegetable Salad

1 (10-ounce) package frozen
  baby lima beans
1 (10-ounce) package frozen cut
  green beans
1 (8-ounce) package process
  cheese, cut into ¼-inch cubes

¾ cup diced celery
3 tablespoons mayonnaise
⅓ cup commercial sour cream
½ teaspoon dill weed
¼ teaspoon salt

Cook vegetables as directed on package; drain and chill. Add cheese and celery to vegetables and mix well. Combine mayonnaise, sour cream, dill weed, and salt; add to vegetable mixture and toss lightly. Yield: 8 servings.

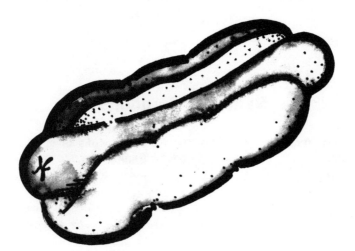

Colonial Apple Pie

1 cup sugar
1 cup unsweetened pineapple juice
8 medium cooking apples, pared
  and sliced
1 tablespoon cornstarch
2 teaspoons water

⅛ teaspoon salt
½ teaspoon vanilla extract
2 teaspoons butter
1 (9-inch) unbaked double
  crust pastry

Combine sugar and juice; bring to a boil over medium heat. Add apple slices; cook slowly, uncovered, until fruit is tender. Lift apples out carefully. Dissolve cornstarch in water; add to syrup mixture. Cook until thick. Add salt, vanilla extract, and butter. Pour over apples in unbaked pastry shell. Cover wtih pastry stips. Bake at 425° for 35 minutes. Yield: 1 (9-inch) pie.

Tangy Punch

½ cup orange-flavored instant
  breakfast drink
¼ cup instant tea mix

4 cups water
5 cups ginger ale

Combine instant breakfast drink, tea mix, and water; stir thoroughly. Add ginger ale and mix well. Yield: 6 to 8 servings.

Backyard Wiener Roast

Dinner for Four to Six

Grilled Wieners

Best Baked Beans

Pretzels

Angels' Halos

Beer

Grilled Wieners

1 (1-pound) package frankfurters
1 package frankfurter rolls
Mustard

Catsup
Pickles
Onions

Roast frankfurters on skewers, sticks, or on grill over medium hot coals. Serve on frankfurter rolls with mustard, catsup, pickles, and onions. Yield: 4 to 6 servings.

Best Baked Beans

1 (1-pound 15-ounce) can pork
and beans
¼ cup catsup
3 tablespoons brown sugar
1 small onion, diced
1 tablespoon dried bacon bits

½ teaspoon chili powder
½ teaspoon dry mustard
Dash red pepper
¼ teaspoon garlic salt
1 medium onion, sliced

Combine all ingredients in greased 1½-quart casserole dish. Stir well and top with onion slices. Bake at 350° for 1 hour. Yield: 4 to 6 servings.

Angels' Halos

½ dozen large
glazed doughnuts

6 large marshmallows

Stick marshmallow in hole of doughnut. Run skewer or pointed green stick through dough-nut and marshmallow. Toast marshmallow care-fully. Yield: 6 servings.

Seafood Dream Dinner

Dinner for Six

Oyster Bake

Shrimp en Brochette

Grilled Corn with Bacon

Fruit Salad Delight

Lemon Pie

Oyster Bake

2 cups seasoned croutons
1 pint shucked oysters, drained
3 tablespoons butter, melted
¼ teaspoon salt
3 tablespoons freshly squeezed lemon juice

1 teaspoon Worcestershire sauce
1 teaspoon chopped parsley
⅓ cup grated Parmesan cheese

Spread croutons in a shallow, greased baking dish; place oysters over croutons. Combine butter, salt, lemon juice, and Worcestershire sauce in small skillet; sauté parsley in this mixture. Spread over oysters. Sprinkle with Parmesan cheese. Cook in smoker or oven at 350° for 24 to 30 minutes, or until oysters are thoroughly heated. Yield: 6 small servings.

Shrimp en Brochette

1½ pounds peeled jumbo shrimp
2 lemons, cut into wedges

Melted butter

Thread large, peeled shrimp on skewers alternating every 1 or 2 shirmp with lemon wedges. Baste with melted butter. Grill about 5 minutes over hot coals, basting wtih butter; turn once. Yield: 6 servings.

Grilled Corn with Bacon

6 ears corn
Seasoned salt

6 strips bacon

Select corn that still has the husks on it. Strip husks back but not off; remove corn silks. Dust corn with seasoned salt and wrap a strip of bacon around ear of corn. Replace the husks and tie securely in place. Cook over charcoal for 15 to 25 minutes until done. Yield: 6 servings.

Fruit Salad Delight

2 bananas, thinly sliced
Powdered sugar
Lime, lemon, or orange juice
2 oranges, cut into thin slices
(seeds and peel removed)
1 pound fresh dark cherries; or
1 (17-ounce) can dark sweet
cherries, pitted

1 pound seedless grapes
1 cantaloupe, cut into chunks;
or watermelon chunks
1 to 2 apples, sliced
2 cups strawberries, halved
1 cup flaked coconut
¾ cup chopped walnuts

Using a large, clear glass bowl, layer banana slices in bottom. Sprinkle lightly with powdered sugar and a squeeze of lime, lemon, or orange juice. Continue to layer all fruit in bowl; be- tween each layer sprinkle powdered sugar and lime, lemon, or orange juice. Top salad with coconut and walnuts; garnish with some of the most colorful fruit. Yield: 6 to 8 servings.

Lemon Pie

1½ cups sugar
Dash salt
⅓ cup cornstarch
1½ cups water
3 egg yolks, slightly beaten
3 tablespoons butter

¼ cup freshly squeezed
lemon juice
1 tablespoon grated lemon rind
1 (9-inch) baked pastry shell
Meringue

Combine sugar, salt, and cornstarch in saucepan; gradually stir in water. Cook over moderate heat, stirring constantly until mixture boils. Boil for 1 minute or until mixture thickens. Sowly stir half the hot mixture into slightly beaten egg yolks. Blend this with re- maining hot mixture. Boil for 1 minute longer, stirring constantly. Remove from heat and con- tinue stirring until smooth. Blend in butter, lemon juice, and lemon rind. Return mixture to heat for 1 or 2 minutes, stirring constantly until firm. Pour into baked pastry shell. Cover with meringue. Yield: 1 (9-inch) pie.

Meringue

3 egg whites
¼ teaspoon cream of tartar

6 tablespoons sugar

Beat egg whites with cream of tartar until frothy; gradually beat in sugar. Continue beat- ing until stiff and glossy. Spread meringue over lemon filling. Seal to edge of crust to prevent shrinking. Bake at 400° until meringue is lightly browned. Yield: enough meringue for 1 (9-inch) pie.

Keep that Book!

Do keep the instruction booklets that come with your equipment, and read them carefully. If you are not sure, or have forgotten a step since you used the equipment last, re-read the suggested method.

Shrimp From the Grill

Dinner for Eight

Oysters-on-the-Rocks

Grilled Shrimp

Foiled French Fries

Cold Vegetable Platter

Double Cheddar Cornbread

Fresh Fruit with Poppy Seed Dressing

French Vanilla Ice Cream

Oysters-on-the-Rocks

Fresh oysters
Salt and pepper
Bacon

Lemon slices
Hot sauce

Shuck and drain oysters, reserving half of shells. Season with salt and pepper. Wrap each oyster with a short strip of bacon and secure with a toothpick. Return wrapped oyster to half-shell and place in hinged wire basket. Grill quickly, turning basket often. Oysters are done when bacon is cooked to desired degree of doneness. Serve with lemon slices and hot sauce.

Grilled Shrimp

2 **pounds large shrimp in shell**
1 **cup salad oil**
1 **cup freshly squeezed lemon juice**
2 **teaspoons Italian dressing mix**
2 **teaspoons seasoned salt**

1 **teaspoon seasoned pepper**
4 **tablespoons brown sugar**
2 **tablespoons soy sauce**
½ **cup chopped green onions**

Peel and devein shrimp, leaving tails intact. Wash shrimp thoroughly; drain on paper towels. Mix together salad oil, lemon juice, salad dressing mix, seasoned salt, and pepper. Place peeled shrimp in bowl and pour marinade over top. Let stand stirring occasionally.

Lift shrimp from marinade with slotted spoon and place on grill about 6 inches from hot coals (use wire basket or string shrimp on skewers). Grill for about 10 minutes, turning once and brushing with marinade.

Pour remaining marinade into pan. Stir in brown sugar, soy sauce, and onions. Heat to boiling. Serve as a dip for shrimp. Yield: 8 servings.

Foiled French Fries

(page 86)

Cold Vegetable Platter

(page 66)

Double Cheddar Cornbread

1 cup yellow cornmeal
1 cup all-purpose flour
3 teaspoons baking powder
1 teaspoon salt
2 cups shredded Cheddar
   cheese, divided
1 cup milk

¼ cup butter, melted
1 egg, beaten
½ teaspoon dry mustard
4 slices bacon, fried crisp
   and crumbled
1 green pepper, cut into rings

Combine cornmeal, flour, baking powder, and salt; stir in 1 cup of cheese. Combine milk, butter, and egg; add to dry ingredients, mixing until blended. Pour into preheated, greased 9-inch skillet. Top with remaining cheese mixed with dry mustard. Sprinkle with bacon, top with green pepper rings. Bake at 425° for 25 to 30 minutes or until golden brown. Yield: 8 to 10 servings.

Fresh Fruit with Poppy Seed Dressing

4 cups combined fresh and drained
   canned fruit

½ to 1 cup Poppy Seed Dressing

Combine fruit and Poppy Seed Dressing just before serving. Serve cold. Yield: 6 to 8 servings.

Poppy Seed Dressing

¼ cup sugar
½ cup white vinegar
1 teaspoon dry mustard
1 teaspoon salt

1 clove garlic, crushed
1 cup salad oil
⅓ large onion, grated
4 teaspoons poppy seed

Combine all ingredients in pint jar. Mix well and chill at least 6 hours before serving.

Yield: 1¼ cups.

French Vanilla Ice Cream

6 egg yolks
2 cups milk
1 cup sugar

¼ teaspoon salt
2 cups whipping cream
1 tablespoon vanilla extract

Beat egg yolks and milk with rotary beater in top of double boiler. Add sugar and salt; cook over simmering water, stirring constantly, until thickened and mixture coats a metal spoon. Let cool, then add cream and vanilla extract. Freeze in electric or hand-turned freezer. Yield: about 1½ quarts.

Hawaiian Lobster Luau

Dinner for Four

Lobster Luau

Mushroom Potatoes

Peas Oriental

Orange Lotus Blossom

Sunny Sundae

Pastel Punch

Lobster Luau

8 lobster tails
¼ cup butter or
  margarine, melted
1 tablespoon dry mustard
1½ teaspoons
  Worcestershire sauce

Juice of 2 lemons
1 (8½-ounce) can pineapple
  tidbits, well-drained
⅓ cup diced celery
¼ cup grated Parmesan cheese

Drop lobster tails into kettle of boiling salted water. Boil for 5 minutes. Drain water and drench with cold water; cut through undershell with scissors. Remove meat and reserve shells; cut meat into bite-size pieces. Combine butter, dry mustard, Worcestershire sauce, and lemon juice; blend well. Add pineapple, celery, and lobster. Put lobster mixture into shells and sprinkle with cheese. Wrap each lobster in a piece of heavy-duty aluminum foil. Grill over medium heat for about 15 minutes. Yield: about 4 servings.

Mushroom Potatoes

(page 52)

Peas Oriental

1 (10-ounce) package frozen peas
½ cup drained and sliced
  water chestnuts

Salt and pepper to taste
3 tablespoons margarine

Break frozen peas apart and combine with water chestnuts. Place on a large square of heavy-duty aluminum foil; season with salt and pepper. Dot with margarine. Wrap foil tightly and bake at 350° for 1 hour or grill over medium heat for 30 to 60 minutes, turning occasionally. Yield: 4 servings.

Orange Lotus Blossom

6 large oranges
1½ cups pitted dark sweet
  cherries, drained
1 (13¼-ounce) can pineapple
  chunks, drained
1½ cups unpeeled apricot
  halves, drained

⅓ cup margarine
4 tablespoons brown sugar
1 teaspoon ground curry powder
  Commercial sour cream

Slice tops from oranges and remove pulp; cut edge in a zigzag pattern around top. Chop orange pulp and combine with cherries, pineapple, and apricots. Fill orange cups with mixed fruit. Combine margarine, brown sugar, and curry powder; sprinkle on top of orange cups. Place each orange on a square of heavy-duty aluminum foil and wrap securely. Grill or bake at 350° for 10 to 15 minutes. Top with sour cream and serve immediately. Yield: 6 servings.

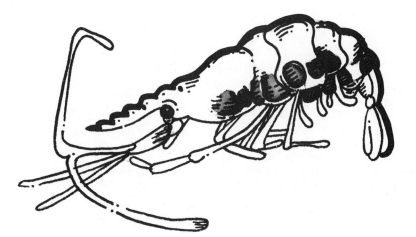

Sunny Sundae

1 pint lime sherbet
1 (8½-ounce) can pineapple
  tidbits, drained

1 (11-ounce) can mandarin orange
  sections, drained
1 cup toasted shredded coconut

Layer sherbet, pineapple, and mandarin oranges in parfait glasses. Repeat layers. Top with coconut. Serve immediately. Yield: 4 to 6 servings.

Pastel Punch

1½ tablespoons red hot
  cinnamon candy
2 tablespoons sugar

¼ cup water
1 pint ginger ale, chilled
3 cups pineapple juice, chilled

Combine candy, sugar, and water in saucepan; stir over low heat until candy melts. Strain and cool. Add chilled ginger ale and pineapple juice. Serve over ice. Yield: about 1½ quarts.

Backyard Fish Festival

Dinner for Four to Six

Broiled Shrimp
Flounder Grilled in Foil
Dilled Yellow Squash
Sour Cream Cole Slaw
Sweet Surprise Soufflé
Corn Cakes

Broiled Shrimp

**1 pound medium-sized
fresh shrimp**

1 pound bacon

Peel shrimp and keep on ice. Cut strips of bacon into four parts, each 2½ inches long. Wrap each shrimp with piece of bacon and secure with a toothpick. Arrange bacon-wrapped shrimp on rack in shallow broiling pan. Broil for 5 minutes or until bacon begins to crisp. Pour off bacon fat from broiling pan. Turn each shrimp over and broil on other side. Serve immediately. Yield: 4 to 6 servings.

Flounder Grilled in Foil

**¼ cup freshly squeezed
lemon juice
4 to 6 pounds flounder*
½ cup thinly sliced onion
4 to 6 stalks celery, chopped
6 medium-size tomatoes, sliced
1 large green pepper, cut
into strips**

**4 carrots, very thinly sliced
¼ cup freshly squeezed
lemon juice
4 to 6 lemon wedges
Butter or margarine
Salt to taste**

Cut four to six squares heavy-duty aluminum foil. Sprinkle ¼ cup lemon juice over flounder; cut fish into four to six serving-size pieces. Put a serving of fish on each square of aluminum foil. On each piece of fish, put sliced onion, chopped celery, sliced tomato, pepper strips, sliced carrots, ¼ cup lemon juice, and lemon wedges. Put a dot of butter on each stack, and add salt to taste. Seal packets securely. Lay on grill over medium heat. Turn packets every 15 minutes, and cook until fish flakes easily, about 35 minutes. Yield: 4 to 6 servings.

* Other types of fish may be used, such as trout, turbot, fish fillets of any kind, mackerel, or red snapper.

Dilled Yellow Squash

1 to 1½ pounds yellow squash
1 large onion, thinly sliced
  Salt and pepper

1 teaspoon snipped fresh dill
  or dill weed
  Butter or margarine

Slice squash into ½-inch slices and place on four to six squares of heavy-duty aluminum foil. Place onion slices on top of squash. Season with salt and pepper and a sprinkling of snipped fresh dill or packaged dill weed. Dot with butter. Seal foil packets and cook over low heat on grill for about 20 minutes, turning often. Yield: 4 to 6 servings.

Sour Cream Cole Slaw

(page 21)

Sweet Surprise Soufflé

2½ cups miniature marshmallows
½ cup milk
3 egg yolks, beaten
2 cups cooked, mashed
  sweet potatoes

2 tablespoons margarine, melted
½ teaspoon salt
½ teaspoon ground nutmeg
3 egg whites, stiffly beaten

Melt marshmallows with milk in top of double boiler; stir until smooth. Gradually add beaten egg yolks; stir and cook for 5 minutes. Combine potatoes, margarine, salt, and nutmeg in a large bowl; add marshmallow mixture, and stir well. Fold in stiffly beaten egg whites. Spoon mixture into 1-cup soufflé dishes or into muffin pans, filling pans half full. Bake at 325° for 30 to 35 minutes. Serve at once. Yield: 4 to 6 servings.

Corn Cakes

1¼ cups regular cornmeal
1 tablespoon all-purpose flour
½ teaspoon salt
½ teaspoon baking powder

½ teaspoon soda
1 egg, slightly beaten
1 cup buttermilk

Combine cornmeal, flour, salt, baking powder, and soda and mix well. Add slightly beaten egg to buttermilk, then stir into cornmeal mixture. Stir just until mixture is well-blended. Drop by spoonfuls onto a hot, well-greased griddle. Cook until mixture bubbles, then turn and cook on other side. Yield: 4 to 6 servings.

Protect the Bottom of Grill

Suggested materials to be used for insulating and preventing soil in the base of the charcoal cooker: first line the bottom with heavy-duty aluminum foil, then place on the foil a layer of oyster shells, non-organic kitty litter, clean sand, or small gravel.

Fish in Foil

Dinner for Six

Grilled Fish Fold-Overs

Onioned Potatoes

Green Bean Casserole

Sliced Fresh Tomatoes or Potato-Cheese Salad

Georgia Hush Puppies

Self-Ice Cake

Grilled Fish Fold-Overs

6 fish fillets
American cheese

Butter or margarine, melted
Salt and pepper

Use sole or other thin fish fillets, fresh or thawed frozen. Make a once-over fold in each fillet, tucking a thin slice of cheese into fold. Brush outside with margarine and sprinkle with salt and pepper. Arrange in close-meshed wire basket and grill quickly over hot coals, turning frequently and brushing with more butter until done. Yield: 6 servings.

Onioned Potatoes

6 medium baking potatoes
½ cup butter or
margarine, softened

1 (1⅜-ounce) package onion
soup mix

Scrub potatoes, but do not pare. Cut each potato into three or four lengthwise slices. Blend butter or margarine and soup mix; spread on slices of potatoes and reassemble potatoes to original shape. Wrap each potato in a square of heavy-duty aluminum foil, overlapping ends. Place on grill over low heat and cook 45 to 60 minutes, turning occasionally. Yield: 6 servings.

Green Bean Casserole

(page 19)

Potato-Cheese Salad

3 cups cooked, diced potatoes
3 hard-cooked eggs, chopped
1 teaspoon salt
¾ cup chopped celery
3 tablespoons grated onion
2 cups diced Cheddar cheese
1 cup commercial sour cream
¼ cup sweet pickle juice
Lettuce

Combine all ingredients except lettuce in given order. Gently toss to combine. Cover and chill for at least 30 minutes for flavors to blend. Serve on lettuce. Yield: 6 servings.

Georgia Hush Puppies

2 cups regular cornmeal
1 tablespoon all-purpose flour
½ teaspoon soda
1 teaspoon baking powder
1 teaspoon salt
1 egg, slightly beaten
3 tablespoons minced onion
1 cup buttermilk
Hot oil

Combine cornmeal, flour, soda, baking powder, and salt in a large bowl. Mix beaten egg, minced onion, and buttermilk together and add to cornmeal mixture; stir well. Drop by spoonfuls into deep hot oil. Fry until brown; remove from oil and drain on paper towels. Yield: 6 servings.

Self-Ice Cake

1 cup chopped dates
1 cup boiling water
1 teaspoon soda
½ cup shortening
1 cup sugar
2 eggs
2 teaspoons cocoa
1 teaspoon vanilla extract
1¾ cups all-purpose flour
½ teaspoon salt
½ teaspoon cream of tartar
1 (6-ounce) package chocolate morsels
¾ cup chopped nuts

Combine dates, water, and soda; let stand until cool. Cream shortening and sugar; add eggs and beat well. Add cocoa and vanilla extract; blend well. Slowly add flour, salt, and cream of tartar; stir until well-blended. Stir in date mixture. Pour into 13- x 9- x 2-inch pan. Sprinkle chocolate morsels and nuts over top of cake. Bake at 350° for 30 minutes. Keep cake covered to store. Yield: 1 (13- x 9- x 2-inch) cake.

Cooking Time Varies

Cooking time for meat will vary with cut, shape, thickness, temperature when placed over coals, temperature of charcoal and distance of meat from charcoal, weather conditions, and degree of doneness desired. Test meat for doneness before taking it off the grill.

Fish Barbecue

Dinner for Eight

Barbecued Stuffed Trout or Whitefish
Roast Corn with Spiced Butter
Mushroom Salad
Garlic-Dill French Bread
Buttermilk Sherbet

Barbecued Stuffed Trout or Whitefish

2 cups soft breadcrumbs
2 cups peeled, chopped cucumbers, squeezed to remove liquid
2 eggs, beaten
½ cup chopped onion
4 tablespoons butter or margarine, melted
½ teaspoon salt
½ teaspoon pepper
1 (4- to 6-pound) trout or whitefish, cleaned and boned
Commercial barbecue sauce
8 slices pineapple, drained
Ripe olives

Combine breadcrumbs, cucumbers, eggs, onion, melted butter or margarine, salt, and pepper; mix well. Stuff the fish and skewer or lace together. Place on a large piece of heavy-duty aluminum foil and brush generously with barbecue sauce. Wrap well and grill over low heat for an hour or longer. Open foil, if fish flakes easily, it is done. Garnish with pineapple slices and ripe olives. Yield: 8 servings.

Roast Corn with Spiced Butter

8 ears corn
½ cup butter, melted
1 teaspoon salt
⅛ teaspoon ground allspice

Pull husks of corn down; remove silk and rinse corn in cold water. Pull husks back up and tie to secure. Put corn on the grill and cook 15 to 20 minutes, turning once or twice. Season butter with salt and allspice; serve with corn. Yield: 8 servings.

Flavoring Olives

Spark up the flavor of ripe olives by soaking them overnight in olive oil to which a small clove of garlic has been added. Make green olives tastier by pouring off the brine, adding 2 tablespoons olive oil, then let stand 30 minutes before using.

Mushroom Salad

1 pound fresh mushrooms
¼ cup freshly squeezed
   lemon juice
6 tablespoons olive oil

1 teaspoon salt
2 teaspoons freshly ground
   black pepper
1 tablespoon chopped parsley

Trim mushroom stems and wipe caps with a damp cloth. Cut mushrooms into thin T-shaped slices. Combine mushrooms, lemon juice, oil, salt, and pepper. Mix well; marinate at room temperature for 1 hour; cover and refrigerate for 1 hour before serving. Sprinkle with parsley and serve. Yield: 8 servings.

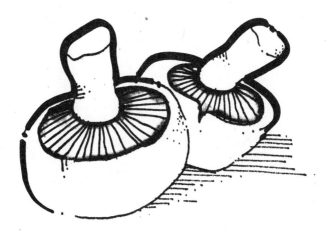

Garlic-Dill French Bread

½ cup butter or
   margarine, softened
1 large clove garlic, crushed
1 teaspoon dried parsley flakes

¼ teaspoon oregano
½ teaspoon dill weed, crushed
1 (1-pound) loaf French bread

Combine butter, garlic, parsley flakes, oregano, and dill weed. Put in covered container and refrigerate. Remove from refrigerator and allow to soften for 1 hour before spreading on bread. Cut bread into ¾-inch slices, but not quite through the bottom crust. Spread butter mixture generously between slices. Wrap loosely in aluminum foil and heat on grill for 15 minutes. Yield: 8 servings.

Buttermilk Sherbet

(page 82)

To Remove Fish Odor

To remove odor from a pan after frying fish, fill pan with vinegar and let come to a boil. Discard vinegar and wash pan in hot soapy water and rinse well.

Barbecued Shrimp Special

Dinner for Eight

Barbecued Shrimp
Potatoes Deluxe
French Cold Vegetable Dish
Foil-Baked Tomatoes with Onion
Chocolate Ice Cream

Barbecued Shrimp

6 large cloves garlic, minced
⅔ cup butter or margarine, melted
2 pounds peeled fresh shrimp

Salt and pepper to taste
2 lemons, thinly sliced
½ cup chopped parsley

Sauté garlic in butter for 2 or 3 minutes. Put layer of shrimp in bottom of a foil pan; season with salt and pepper. Put lemon slices over shrimp; drizzle with garlic butter and sprinkle with parsley. Cook over hot coals for 8 to 10 minutes or until done. Turn shrimp frequently. Yield: 8 servings.

Potatoes Deluxe

1 (8-ounce) carton commercial
**   sour cream**
¾ cup milk
1 (1¼-ounce) package sour cream
**   sauce mix**

3 cups boiled, diced potatoes
**   Salt and pepper to taste**
½ cup buttered breadcrumbs
¼ cup grated Parmesan cheese

Heat (do not boil) sour cream; combine milk and sour cream sauce mix, and blend well with sour cream. Layer diced potatoes and sour cream mixture in greased 1½-quart casserole dish; repeat layers. Sprinkle with salt and pepper, cover with buttered bread-crumbs, and top with Parmesan cheese. Bake at 350° for 30 minutes or until crumbs are brown and casserole is bubbly. Yield: 8 servings.

To Keep Food Warm

If you don't have an electric serving tray for keeping food hot, nest bowls of sauces, cas-seroles, or meat in heated rock salt to keep them warm until serving time.

French Cold Vegetable Dish

1 (16-ounce) can French-style
   green beans, drained
1 (16-ounce) can tiny
   peas, drained
1 small onion, minced
½ green pepper, chopped
1 pimiento, chopped
2 stalks celery, diced

1 teaspoon paprika
   Salt and pepper to taste
1 cup vinegar
½ cup salad oil
1 cup sugar
1 (16-ounce) can tiny whole
   beets, drained
1 cup shredded cabbage

Combine beans, peas, onion, green pepper, pimiento, celery, paprika, salt and pepper; mix well and set aside. Combine vinegar, salad oil, and sugar to make dressing; place over low heat, stirring constantly until sugar is dissolved. Marinate bean-pea mixture in 1½ cups dressing and use remaining dressing to marinate beets in a separate bowl. Chill both bowls of vegetables overnight. Before serving, drain all vegetables and mix with cabbage. Yield: 8 to 10 servings.

Foil-Baked Tomatoes with Onion

Tomatoes
Salt and pepper

Onion

Select medium, firm tomatoes (one tomato per person). Cut each tomato in half crosswise; sprinkle cut surfaces with salt and pepper and put together again, placing a thin slice of onion between tomato halves. Use a toothpick to hold the reassembled tomato intact. Wrap each tomato in a 6-inch square of heavy-duty aluminum foil. Cook at edge of grill for 15 to 20 minutes.

Chocolate Ice Cream

1¼ cups sugar
8 egg yolks, beaten
4 ounces sweet chocolate, grated

1 quart milk, scalded
1 teaspoon vanilla extract
1 cup whipping cream

Combine sugar, egg yolks, and chocolate in top of double boiler. Add scalded milk and cook, stirring constantly, about 3 to 5 minutes. Cool. Add vanilla extract and cream. Chill. Pour into chilled freezer container and freeze. Yield: ½ gallon.

Good Potato Salad

Potato salad is better if you marinate the potatoes with French or Italian dressing, onions, and green peppers for several hours before adding mayonnaise. You might add pimiento, hard-cooked eggs, or other seasonings to marinade. Add mayonnaise just before serving.

Southern Seafare Spread

Dinner for Eight

Cheese-Stuffed Fish Fillets

Garden Row Casserole

Harvest Slaw

Skillet Corn Cakes

Lemon Ripple

Cheese-Stuffed Fish Fillets

1 (4-pound) or 2 (2-pound) fish, dressed and boned
½ cup butter or margarine, divided
½ cup chopped onion
¼ cup chopped green pepper

1 teaspoon salt
Dash pepper
2 cups dry breadcrumbs
6 tablespoons shredded American cheese

Cut fish into eight pieces. Melt ⅓ cup butter. Sauté onion and green pepper in butter until tender; add seasonings and breadcrumbs. Cut eight squares of heavy-duty aluminum foil. Spread center of each foil square with remaining butter and sprinkle with 1 tablespoon cheese.

Place a piece of fish on cheese, skin-side down; cover with ¼ cup stuffing. Wrap fish in a tight foil packet. Grill 3 to 4 inches above medium heat for 10 to 12 minutes; turn and cook an additional 10 to 12 minutes. Serve from foil. Yield: 8 servings.

Garden Row Casserole

1 (10¾-ounce) can cream of chicken soup
1 cup shredded American cheese
¼ teaspoon salt
½ cup milk
2 (16-ounce) cans tiny whole potatoes, drained

2 (16-ounce) bottles whole onions, drained
1 (16-ounce) can green peas, drained
1 cup buttered breadcrumbs

Combine soup, cheese, salt, and milk; stir over low heat until well-blended. Add vegetables and mix well. Pour into greased 3-quart cas- serole dish. Top with breadcrumbs. Bake at 350° for 25 minutes or until bubbly. Yield: 8 to 10 servings.

Protect Your Pans

If you are using a pan directly on heat, rub outside generously with soap before placing over the fire.

Harvest Slaw

1 medium head cabbage, shredded
2 carrots, shredded
1 green pepper, finely diced

1 medium onion, finely diced
Dressing for Slaw

Combine cabbage, carrots, green pepper, and onion in large bowl. Toss with dressing. Cover and refrigerate; slaw keeps well in refrigerator for several days. Yield: 10 to 12 servings.

Dressing for Slaw

1¼ cups vinegar
1 cup sugar
¾ teaspoon mustard seed

½ teaspoon turmeric
½ teaspoon salt

Heat vinegar; add sugar, mustard seed, turmeric, and salt. Stir over low heat until mixture is dissolved. Cool dressing and pour over slaw. Yield: about 2 cups.

Skillet Corn Cakes

1 cup salad oil
1½ cups cornmeal
⅓ cup all-purpose flour
2 teaspoons baking powder

½ teaspoon salt
½ cup milk
1 egg, beaten
1 cup cream-style corn

Heat salad oil in heavy skillet. Combine cornmeal, flour, baking powder, and salt; add milk, egg, and corn. Mix well. Fry heaping tablespoons of batter in hot oil until golden brown, adding more oil if needed. Serve hot. Yield: about 2 dozen cakes.

Lemon Ripple

2 cups graham cracker crumbs
2 tablespoons sugar
3 tablespoons butter or
** margarine, softened**

1 (6-ounce) can frozen lemonade
** concentrate, partially thawed**
1 quart vanilla ice cream,
** slightly softened**

Combine graham cracker crumbs, sugar, and butter; mix well and press crumbs evenly and firmly in bottom of 9-inch square pan, reserving 2 tablespoons of crumb mixture for topping. Chill crust. Ripple lemonade concentrate through ice cream. Spoon into chilled crumb crust. Top with reserved crumbs and freeze until firm. Cut into squares. Yield: 8 to 10 servings.

Douse That Flame!

A clothes sprinkler or a squirt bottle sold for catsup or mustard makes a good water holder for squirting on flames that flare up from fat cooking on the charcoal fire.

Index